From Luby's to the Legislature

❖ ❖ ❖

One Woman's Fight Against Gun Control

FROM LUBY'S TO THE LEGISLATURE

ONE WOMAN'S FIGHT AGAINST GUN CONTROL

Suzanna Gratia Hupp

Privateer Publications
San Antonio, Texas

Privateer Publications, 1 (210) 308-8191
Post Office Box 29427, San Antonio, TX 78229 USA

Printed in the United States of America.
Impression 10 9 8 7 6 5 4 3 2 1
Library of Congress Control Number: 2009907752

**Publisher's Cataloging-in-Publication
(Provided by Quality Books, Inc.)**

    Hupp, Suzanna Gratia.
       From Luby's to the legislature : one woman's fight
      against gun control / Suzanna Gratia Hupp.
       p. cm.
       ISBN-13: 978-0-9656784-4-5
       ISBN-10: 0-9656784-4-X

       1. Hupp, Suzanna Gratia. 2. Women legislators--Texas
    --Biography. 3. Firearms--Law and legislation--Texas--
    History--20th century. 4. Firearms ownership--
    Government policy--Texas--20th century. 5. Gun control
    --Texas--History--20th century. 6. Mass murder--Texas--
    Killeen--Biography. 7. Texas. Legislature. House of
    Representatives--Biography. 8. United States.
    Constitution.--2nd Amendment--History--20th century.
    I. Title.

    HV7437.T4H87 2009   363.3'3'09764
                       QBI09-600081

Credits: The author and publisher thank the Houston Chronicle for
permission to use the front page of the *Houston Post* for October 17, 1991,
on the cover of this book. Copyright © 1991 Houston Chronicle Publishing
Company. Reprinted with permission. All rights reserved.
  They also thank the Center for American History at The University of Texas at
Austin for providing the image used and the Killeen Daily Herald for permission to use the photographs taken at Luby's Cafeteria on October 16, 1991.
  The book cover was designed and produced by Tom Hudgins; Kemp Davis
took the photograph; and Susan Hughes, Wordwright Associates, was the
editor and layout designer.
Usage Note: Use of the masculine pronoun is not intended to be
discriminatory.

This book is dedicated to my parents,
Al and Ursula (Suzy) Gratia

As well as the other innocent victims
of the Luby's Massacre
and the many other crimes
in which so-called gun-control laws
have left people defenseless.

CONTENTS

Foreword

Few people's life stories matter much for public policy debates, but the horrible tragedy Suzanna Hupp endured at the Luby's Cafeteria in 1991 is something no one should have to face. Suzanna, who lost both her parents in that senseless attack, has spent much of her life trying to prevent similar tragedies from happening to others. That event led her to be a nationally recognized speaker and to become a powerful committee chairman in the Texas State Legislature. Suzanna's eloquence and drive that are so apparent on the pages of this book explain why she has made such a difference in the national debate over gun ownership and the Second Amendment.

The book provides a moving personal story from a horrible tragedy to triumphs that make Suzanna the person she is. We read about the life lessons that helped to shape her strong belief systems. From her childhood experiences with her family to the halls of the Texas State Capitol and beyond, the remarkable story reminds us that life often goes down roads that no one could have expected and that ultimately we are each responsible for our own safety and security.

No one would have thought that the young Suzanna, a chiropractor and horsewoman, would one day be testifying before Congress and multiple state legislatures around the country. I have seen that testimony first hand and been impressed by the powerful effect it had on those who heard it. No one would have guessed that she would be thrust into the national and even international spotlight as she began regular appearances on national news shows in the U.S., as well as garnering news coverage around the world. She continues to be quoted in publications as diverse as the *Wall Street Journal*, *Time*, and *People* magazine. Her experiences were even discussed in the Heller case, in which the Supreme Court ruled that the right to keep and bear arms is an individual right.

Since that terrible day in 1991, the U.S. and countries around the world have gone on to witness a seemingly endless supply of madmen seeking to leave their mark by slaughtering defenseless people. Yet, many do not like the idea of citizens carrying handguns, and the debate about whether to allow law-abiding citizens the ability to protect themselves is as polarizing as ever. Suzanna forces us to face these horrible incidents on a human level as only someone who has lived through it can. The book is more than just a compilation of life stories about an extremely interesting person. Suzanna's useful insights into how politics and politicians operate serve as a guide to the citizen lobbyist. A lot of lessons in life are in here for those who take the time to read it. This is a powerful book, and I suspect it will change a lot of minds about the right to self-defense.

John R. Lott, Jr.
Economist and author of
The Bias against Guns and *More Guns Less Crime*

Acknowledgements and Apologies

I should make it clear from the outset that I had no great, burning desire to write a book. The following pages were essentially wrought from me by the many Second Amendment crusaders who, having heard my story, wanted something in written form that they could pass on to the "non-believers" and "fence-sitters" of their acquaintance. I owe those folks a large debt of gratitude for encouraging me to actually sit down and work through this rather grueling process. I must it admit it was, at times, cathartic.

It should also be clarified that I do not hold this book out to be a journalistic effort with facts and figures, timelines and police reports. This is a narrative of MY recollections of thoughts, emotions, and events that have shaped my belief system regarding guns. I went out of my way to eliminate some names and specifics in an effort to avoid bogging the reader down with minutia that is irrelevant to the heart of this matter. Besides, many books have been written about the Second Amendment, firearms, and the Luby's massacre that already contain every bit of factual tidbit you could ever want to know, and written by far better historians than I could ever hope to be. I could see no reason to rehash those reports.

In keeping with that purpose, you will also note one other glaring omission: I never give you the name of the man who murdered my parents and many others at the restaurant that day. There is no doubt in my mind that part of the reason he did what he did was to have his name up in lights, so to speak. That pathetic monster wanted it in the newspapers and history books so it would be remembered forevermore. I refuse to be a party to his diabolical plot. If you have to know, you can look it up on the Internet.

I would like to personally thank all of the "first-responders" to that fateful October shooting. Those brave men and women saved lives, while in some cases, risking their own. More than a couple of officers and paramedics have told me that their own lives were changed forever by what they witnessed or encountered. One of the first guys on the scene told me that he had seen worse in Vietnam, but that this affected him differently: he could "compartmentalize" the savagery of war. But, he was caught completely unprepared for this kind of carnage in his "own backyard." He had never expected to see bodies of innocent friends and acquaintances strewn about him in a local restaurant. I think that in our overwhelming concern for the immediate victims, we forget about the "psychological casualties" that occur in our professionals. My hat's off to those who have used their experiences to help train others to deal with similar emergencies.

I also owe a debt of gratitude to my publisher, Chris Bird, for he believes so deeply in my cause that he took on the monumental task of working with me and my flooded schedule.

Since my brother Allan is five years older than me, I am pretty sure that upon reading some of my childhood remembrances he will likely exclaim, "That's not how that happened!" To which I would reply, "Tough! That's how I remember it!" My younger sister, Erika, will probably have similar comments regarding her parts of the story.

To both siblings and their respective spouses, Kathy and Buddy, I want to express my love and beg their indulgence for my (undoubtedly) skewed memories.

To my children, Alex and Ethan: You are probably the real driving force behind the writing of this book. I want you to understand why you never got to know your (maternal) grandparents. It is such a loss, they were really neat people. Most of all, I have penned this so that you have a deep and personal understanding of what it means to have a legislature take away your right to defend your-selves and your future families.

And it is with greatest love, appreciation, and respect that I want to acknowledge my husband, Greg, without whose encouragement, love, and ongoing tech support, this book would never have been completed!

Suzanna Gratia Hupp

PROLOGUE

I cannot remember when the recurrent dreams started… perhaps when I was a teenager. Well, not recurrent dreams exactly, more of a recurrent theme to my dreams. Once or twice a month they would crop up. They were unsettling, although they did not even live up to the title of "nightmares." There was no jerking awake into a sitting position, with heart palpitating and the sheets soaking wet. It was more of a slow awakening, where I would roll over and look at the clock, feeling more annoyed than terrified.

They would start with different story lines: often interesting or even exciting, like an episode of a good cop show. But they would always end in essentially the same way: somehow I would find myself in a situation where I could take out the bad guy, be the hero, and save the day. But, I would typically have to put myself into some vulnerable position to do it. As I would bravely step out from behind cover and raise my revolver to take a bead on the scumbag, he would spot me and, in dreamy slow motion, turn to face me. At the same time, I could see his muscles flex as he would swing the barrel of his gun into line with my torso.

But I was confident. The element of surprise was already in my favor, and I had him perfectly sighted in. I slowly and smoothly tightened my finger against the trigger.

Then it happened.

My finger hit a dead end. At the point when I should have felt the hammer snap forward and the firing pin hit home, when my grip should have been feeling the recoil and my ears ringing from the blast, when the bad guy should be staggering backwards with a bloody hole in his shoulder from my bullet, there is…nothing. My gun simply would not fire. There I stood, unable to defend myself, vulnerable.

I cannot tell you what happened next because I always woke up...greatly annoyed.

CHAPTER I
Growing Up Gratia

I did not grow up in a house with guns.

Well, that is assuming you are not one of those people who believe a child should be expelled from school because he has a three-inch-long, lime-green squirt gun in his backpack. Of course that also doesn't count the dime-store versions of the Lone Ranger's six-shooters, or the Rifleman's really cool lever-action rifle, or any of a myriad of other toy guns we role-played with on a daily basis.

Oh, how I loved galloping around on my stick horse with a cowboy hat on my head and "pearl-handled" revolvers riding low on my hips. When my mother would tolerate it, they would be "loaded" with rolls of caps that would add to the great illusion my brother Allan and I were creating. The good guy would always win, and morality would prevail.

Then there was the Christmas when my ten-year-old brother got a BB gun. (Okay, maybe I did grow up in a

That's me in a diaper and cowboy hat with a six-shooter at my side, posing with my brother Allan.

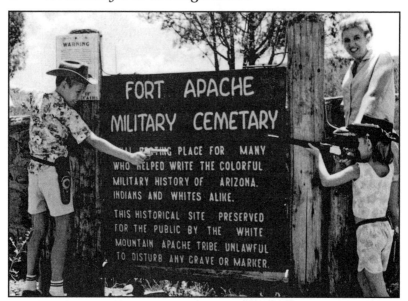

*Allan, Mom, and me posing in front of a historical site in my
birth state of Arizona. No doubt Dad was behind the camera.*

house with a gun…at least briefly.) I was five at the time,
and I remember tagging along when my father and mother
took him out on the Arizona desert near our home to teach
him the rules of firearm ownership. I do not really recall
them teaching him how to shoot, but I have specific memories of Dad showing Allan how to safely hold and carry
that Red Ryder. And there was no horseplay.

We used to love to go out into what seemed like the
middle of nowhere. We would rock hunt, play Cowboys
and Indians, search for wild-animal bones, and plink. We
loved to plink. The ability to aim that BB gun at tin cans
and other discarded trash and actually make them jump
around (or in my case, kick the dust up around them)
was great fun. The inevitable little metallic thump heard
when the BB hits its mark makes it easy to understand the
activity's nickname. Of course this was always carried out
under the watchful eye of one or both parents.

We did not go after live targets. It just wasn't in our
collective psyche. Neither my Mom nor Dad hunted, but

there was never any question about guns being a good and healthy pastime. It wasn't until years later I learned my father could not bear to be the cause of any pain or suffering to any of God's creatures. Later in his life he gave up fishing for the same reason. However, he would not hesitate to come to our defense in any way necessary.

Then one day the unthinkable happened.

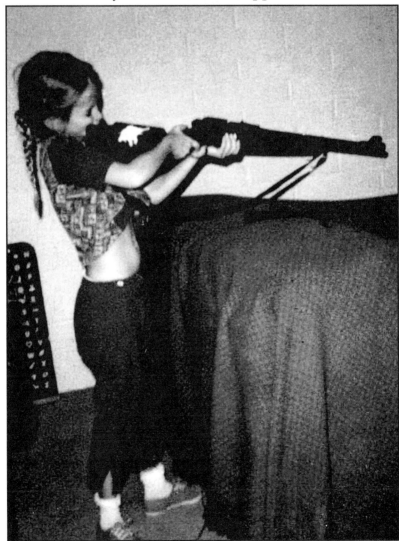

Playing with my brother's new "elephant gun."

I can remember being home on a very cold day while Allan was out by himself with the BB gun, a privilege he had fought hard to earn. I remember hearing not a knock, but an odd pounding, on the front door. After hearing Allan's voice, I opened it. There stood my brother in a heavy winter coat, shivering. The reason he had not simply turned the doorknob and entered was held very gingerly in his gloved hands. It was a dove, still alive, but shot in the neck with a BB. I watched silently as he laid that dying bird on a TV tray he had me quickly assemble. He found a pair of tweezers near my mother's make-up mirror and carefully sterilized them with the flame from a match. Then, on that makeshift surgical table, he did his best to save the doomed creature. At the time, I think he believed his very soul might be at stake.

Of course, the poor bird died, and I don't think either of us breathed a word about the incident to our parents for years. Mom said she found the BB gun months later, behind my brother's dresser. She had wrongly assumed he had merely lost interest in it. As far as I know, he never touched it again.

That was my only early experience with a "real" gun. The main points I brought forward with me were how to hold, carry, and load a firearm safely. And, most importantly, if you point it at something, that "something" might die. And you would have killed it. To this day, I think those are very valuable lessons.

❖ ❖ ❖

CHAPTER 2
Wounded

As I grew, I continued to play Cowboys and Indians, Cops and Robbers, and various forms of Army with my older brother. We had all manner of play guns: there were squirt guns and pop guns, "Tommy" guns and Winchesters, German semi-automatics and an elephant gun with sights. My personal favorites, though, were still the "pearl-handled" set of Colt six-shooters that hung from a belt in their fringed-leather holsters. There is a picture of me in diapers with a cowboy hat on my head, too-big boots on my toddler feet, and those six-shooters on my hips. I think I had just shot Black Bart on his stick horse (feigning death, my brother lay at my feet).

My favorite television shows were those with horses, good guys catching bad guys, and horses. (That is not an editing error. Horses clearly needed to be on the list twice, just as they were on the list of fictional Colonel Potter—of M*A*S*H fame—when he described what made a movie

Decked out in TV-western garb, that's me standing over the vanquished bad guy (Allan).

great.) Guns were merely something the good guys used to catch the bad guys or protect innocents. A vital prop, to be sure, but to me they were secondary. The best shows were still "The Rifleman," "The Lone Ranger," "Bonanza," and "The Wild, Wild West." We acted them out in our western garb, all the while learning Good from Evil and that decency and courage would always win the day.

My next encounter with a real gun came shortly after we moved to Texas, when I was about nine-years-old. My parents had gone on a brief grocery-shopping trip and left my two-year-old-sister Erika and me in our older brother's care. We had wandered down to a little bridge that crossed an irrigation canal where we delighted in trying to catch big alligator-gar fish in our hand-held dip nets. I'm not sure we ever caught one, but it was great fun trying. Erika watched us from a position of safety, snugly strapped into her stroller. A few other local kids began showing up to fish or just goof off in the summer sun.

At some point in the comings and goings, one young boy of about twelve showed up with a pellet gun. He was one of the few kids, in our somewhat isolated neighborhood, whom we did not know very well. I knew Allan was not particularly fond of him after an incident that had occurred some weeks earlier. Apparently, the boy had been out on that same bridge shooting at a couple of herons while they were performing a mating ritual: more of a dance, really. He had not hit his mark, but my brother had admonished him and shooed both him and the birds off. I am sure he wasn't a bad kid, just one who lacked parental involvement or supervision and desperately needed it.

The Accidental Shootist

In this case he seemed to be sticking to wreaking havoc on inanimate objects in the creek bed beneath the bridge. Of course, passing a loaded gun from one person to another is nearly always a bad practice. But that is exactly what occurred when that kid handed the gun to Kevin, another neighborhood boy whom we knew pretty well. What he apparently did not do was warn Kevin that the gun had a hair trigger. Just the lightest squeeze would set it off.

Call it being in the wrong place at the wrong time: Kevin touched the trigger, the gun went off, and I was the unlucky barrier to the bullet traveling more than about a dozen feet. I vividly remember what it felt like to have that pellet find its way into my arm. I did not immediately feel pain: I felt impact. It was as if Superman had thwacked me with his middle finger really hard. My mouth hung open in that stupid, startled, gasping look people get when they have been really surprised.

A moment later I looked down at my arm and saw blood trickling from a small hole in the meaty side of my right elbow. That was when I lost it. That was when everyone else lost it. Everyone, that is, except my brother. He immediately went into action, grabbed me by that arm and began running, with me in tow, to the closest house, wiping the blood from my wound with his hand as we went.

The closest house happened to be that of the accidental shootist. I was fortunate that Kevin's mother stayed calm while she washed my arm in the bathroom sink and tried to locate the pellet. I thought she would kill one of the other boys who stuck his head into the room and very seriously asked, "Will she live?" Out in the living room, my poor brother finally flopped down into an armchair and began to take a breath. Suddenly he realized that in our panicked flight, Erika had been left where she was. Another boy was quickly dispatched to retrieve the child, who was found still snuggly strapped into the stroller, on the bridge overlooking the creek, asleep.

It was pointed out by all involved that a guardian angel must have been hard at work that day. For if the bullet had gone just a few inches to my left, it would have hit my sister in the head, instead of me in the arm.

After everyone settled down and it was determined the wound was indeed not life threatening, Allan and I walked the short distance home, with Erika still blissfully snoozing in her carriage. Once there, Allan made me lie down on the couch with a clean, cool cloth to my wound, and we waited for our folks to get home.

In the days before cell phones the short wait seemed an eternity. But eventually we heard the car pull into the driveway, and my brother rushed to meet our parents at the door. In his seemingly reasonable desire to quickly allay their fears, but still convey the message, he said the worst possible thing: "Mom. Dad. Don't worry, but Suzy's been shot."

"What!" they shrieked in stereo.

Fortunately, they had me in sight within just a moment or two and instantly knew no vital organs were at stake. A trip to the local doctor and an x-ray confirmed the pellet was deep in my elbow tissue. Thirty minutes of painful digging around could not locate that pesky hunk of lead, and so the hole was simply stitched closed. The worst part of the whole experience came a few weeks later. You see, it was Easter time: the one time of the year I got to go out with Mom and buy an outfit for church. That year's choice was a beauty, too: a gorgeous pink frou-frou gown with a big, lacy petticoat, pink patent-leather shoes, pink purse, and an Easter bonnet to die for. That darned doctor, after stitching me up, pulled out a hideous, huge, black sling and said, "She'll have to wear this for a while."

Now it was my turn. "What!" I exclaimed with tears streaming down my face. I began begging for any other color. I would have even taken a big, white cast over that gosh-awful thing. But I was stuck with it.

Moms have an amazing way of making things all better, though. Another picture in our album is of the family on Easter Sunday, posing in front of Hope Lutheran Church. I am in all of my finery and, yes, I have a big,

*The whole family in front of the church on Easter morning:
Dad, me, Allan, Erika, and Mom. Note the brooch Mom placed
on the ugly sling that held my wounded arm.*

black, ugly sling on. But in the middle of the sling is one of my mother's beautiful, pink, and very grown-up brooches. I was happy.

Many weeks after the stitches were removed, the pellet migrated around to the point of my elbow and could be felt just under my skin. It was really cool to be able to entertain my third grade friends by grasping it and moving it around. My really good friends got to take turns feeling it. Unfortunately, it got me another trip to the doctor. One small incision and two stitches later, I was pellet-free, darn it. That would have been OK, except I promptly lost the small, bloody trophy I planned to exhibit as the best Show-and-Tell prop ever! Double darn it!

CHAPTER 3
Dad and the Bill of Rights

My junior-high, high-school, and early-college years were spent locked in philosophical battles with my father beyond the normal teenage trials. Dad had begun the slow process of writing a very technical, footnoted book suggesting some major changes he believed should be made in the way our federal government is run; changes he insisted would bring us back to the intent of our Founders.

He had spent many years poring over old books, new books, and the Founders' own writings, and had become quite an expert on our country's beginnings. The library he had acquired over the decades filled one room of the small apartment we shared with my mother and sister. Allan had married and was off on his own. But Dad was able to regale Erika and me with fascinating stories of our country's Founders. They were so much more entertaining than the amazingly boring excuse for history I was being spoon-fed in the public school.

Don't get me wrong. Relatively speaking, I went to a terrific school, but history and its cousin "social studies" typically got relegated to being coach-taught. Every sports coach was required by some well-meaning, but shortsighted, state law to teach at least one substantive course. For some strange reason, history usually won out. Although they may have been the finest football coaches in the world, they were typically dreadful in the classroom. (I do recall one exception to that rule: Coach Renfro. I was fortunate enough to have him for a couple of high-school history-type courses. He was truly an enigma.) Most of the teachers spouted only what they had been taught in the colleges and universities they had attended, or merely the curriculum the school laid out for them.

So as I was being fed liberal half-truths and rewritten history at school, my father was cluttering up my mind with facts at home. Naturally, the two would often clash. I even recall a time when he actually invited my junior-high social-studies teacher to our home for dinner—horror of horrors—and a chat. It worked out quite well in the end, but I do not think my body ever digested that meal.

Over the next several years, I think Dad became frustrated with his inability to briefly summarize parts of his book when chatting with small groups. It bothered him so much he joined a chapter of Toastmasters and spent many months working through their program with great zeal.

Dad eventually became adroit at public speaking as well as writing. He practiced summarizing his thoughts and putting them on paper and quickly became a regular contributor of articles to the newspaper in El Paso where we lived in the early '80s. He wrote serious essays to voice his views of current events as they related to our Constitution or other founding documents.

Sometimes he wrote silly articles to satirize an issue and clarify it for the readers. One brief Letter to the Editor that was published spoke of a relatively new organization called Mothers Against Drunk Driving. They wanted sobriety checkpoints in Texas that are now quite common in other states. Dad believed (and I agree) those check points are a gross violation of our Fourth Amendment right to be free from warrantless searches and from being stopped without probable cause.

Instead of addressing it directly, which he had done in other articles, he spoke of the many accidents or near-accidents he had personally seen caused by women applying makeup while operating a motor vehicle. In fact, he asserted, he was forming a group to combat this dangerous trend: DAMN—Dads Against Makeup Nuts. Needless to say, it rattled a few cages.

It was during those years I came to truly understand the meaning of the first ten amendments to our Constitution, known simply as The Bill of Rights. Although there was not a gun in our house at that time, my grasp of the Second Amendment had become solid. I knew exactly where it stood in importance for maintaining a free nation and individual liberty, as well as how vital that right is to the protection of something else everyone can comprehend: self.

Note: See appendices for text of the Declaration of Independence, the Bill of Rights, and a letter from Dad to an El Paso newspaper.

CHAPTER 4
Good Advice from a Prosecutor

At the ripe old age of nineteen, I set off to make my own way back to my birth state of Arizona. A dear friend of mine who is a veterinarian in Texas helped me make the move across three states to my new home in Tucson. Shortly after arrival, he introduced me to an old friend who happened to be a gunsmith. Before I knew it, the two of them had me out on the desert again, plinking. This time it was with bigger, more powerful handguns. I was not a particularly good shot then (nor am I now), but I could usually hit what I aimed at. And it was so much fun!

Within weeks, and thanks to the generosity of my vet friend, I was the proud owner of a Dan Wesson .357 Magnum revolver. Good for plinking and home defense. I must admit that one or two times it felt good to have that pistol in my hand when some weirdo came beating on my door late at night calling some guy's name. It was a flimsy little apartment door, and the nice policeman did not show up for forty-five minutes.

Incidents like that helped me realize that I did not want to live in a cheap apartment forever. I started taking college courses again, and a few years later I moved to Pasadena, Texas, to complete my Doctor of Chiropractic degree.

Of course, like any good college student, I began dating another doctor-to-be, who held a part-time job and could afford to splurge on dinner and a movie now and then. His employer turned out to be the ex-cop father of one of my old high-school friends, and he owned a terrific little gun and tackle shop. It did not take long before these two conspired to arm me with a .38 caliber Smith and Wesson Airweight and a specialized purse in which to tote it.

Allan and I at our graduation from Texas Chiropractic College.

At that time, in the state of Texas, it was illegal to carry a firearm, concealed or otherwise, on one's person. Even though the rest of the world thought of us as a gun-totin' kind of place, the laws in New York state were actually more lax in this regard. So it was not with a great deal of joy or comfort that I joined the ranks of people who carried illegally, believing an unjust law — when obeying it carries a threat to my life and limb — could be justly, albeit carefully, ignored. I was one of the Good Guys, after all! I did not carry my firearm with me at all times and in all situations, but because of its presence, I generally walked and moved with more confidence and self-assuredness: those subtle indicators predators recognize and avoid.

I carried it intermittently throughout my college years and after graduation. It was not until I had gotten my license to practice chiropractic and was associating at a clinic in the heart of Houston that I became somewhat enlightened. One of my patients, who, for reasons that should be obvious, will remain anonymous, was an assistant district attorney with many interesting stories to tell.

When the subject of guns came up one day, I explained to him my situation and my nasty little habit of "sometimes" carrying my revolver. Fully expecting to be chastised for my breach of the law, I was instead shocked by his admonition to carry it "always" and "in a loaded and quickly reachable place." He went so far as to say I should make a habit of having it out of my purse and in my hand every time I entered my home. I should also do a quick "walk-through" to check possible hiding places.

The old peek-behind-the-shower-curtain thing seemed a bit paranoid to me, but when I said so, he replied, "Suzy, you grew up in a nice area and didn't see a lot of violence. But it's out there, and I see it everyday. Sometimes all it takes is a little vigilance and planning to prevent the unthinkable. You lock your doors don't you?"

"Yes."

"Is that being paranoid? Well, I can pop the lock off a door or get through a window in less than ten seconds… and I'm not a professional. Don't get me wrong; locking your door is important. You want to put as many blocks between you and the bad guys as possible. But, let's play 'What If' for a minute. What if you're in bed and someone breaks through a window and had taken the five seconds needed to cut the phone line first?"

That night in Arizona when some drunk guy was banging on my apartment door and the subsequent forty-five minute wait for the police quickly came to mind.

"What are you going to do? What if you hear a suspicious noise when you come home at night, and when you pull back the shower curtain, someone really is there? Are you prepared?

"Let me tell you I practice what I preach. No, I'm not paranoid. But I have seen the results of people who live with their heads in the sand and think the cops will take care of them. Sometimes the police get lucky, but most of the time they're just the cleanup crew."

He picked up his coat and his white Stetson and left the treatment room. I was dumbfounded. I never wanted to be a victim. His speech changed my life.

CHAPTER 5
A Gun in the Hand

For years I went along with a new mindset. I dutifully carried my .38 on a daily basis and made some effort to be more vigilant at home. I paid more attention to where I parked my car, both at my apartment complex and away from home. I always opted for a well-lit area, away from potential hiding places such as dumpsters, alleys, bushes, vans, or SUVs. I made it a habit to glance into the back seat and at the floorboard of my car before I got into it. (That was something my mother had preached for as long as I could remember.)

When I arrived home, I would take a moment to scan the windows and doors for any signs of tampering. Once I was inside, I would take a quick walk-through to check potential hiding places for visitors. I did not cultivate these habits out of fear or paranoia. To my way of thinking, it was no different than checking the batteries in my smoke alarms. Those were simple things I could do to increase my level of safety.

Occasionally, circumstances occurred in which having a gun handy gave me great comfort. I never had to display or brandish it, but I truly believe the extra confidence it allowed me to have may actually have prevented some situations from escalating into something more dangerous.

Most creeps who are out looking to create mayhem simply do not want to put themselves on the line. Just like predators in the wild, they invariably look for animals that act like prey: the old, the young, the weak, the stumbling, the frail, the sick, etc. They do not go after something that looks as if it could defend itself or potentially inflict some bodily injury on them in return.

Any woman who has ever taken a class in self defense knows one of the most important things she can do to ward off a possible attack is to walk with confidence: head held high, aware of her surroundings, with strides that are strong and certain, movements that are clear and decisive, such as having car keys out and ready. It is an attitude that says, "I see you. I know what you are about. I will not be an easy victim. Look elsewhere."

I cannot imagine there is one of you reading this book who has not seen this scenario played out on the plains of the Serengeti in some National Geographic-type documentary dozens of times, minus the car keys. As much as we would like to think we have become far more advanced, let me remind you there are still predators among us.

Even though I had never displayed or used my gun, with one small exception I will share with you later, there were many times when I was temporarily stuck in a bad situation made safer because of the presence of my firearm.

A Long, Dark Drive

One event in particular stands out in my mind. I was driving by myself from my home in central Texas to Albuquerque, New Mexico, to attend the last few days of that year's Arabian Horse National Championships. It was about a ten-hour drive I knew very well, and I had a nice little Mercedes that was the first evidence of the long hours I had been spending at my new clinic in Copperas Cove, Texas.

It was about 9 o'clock on a Sunday night. I was on a stretch of Interstate 40 two or three hours out of Albuquerque. It was absolutely desolate, made more so by a treacherous wind that whipped out of the north and buffeted my little car continuously. Nevertheless, I was making good time and looking forward to being in a hotel room very soon, when I slowly became aware I was having trouble seeing the highway before me. My headlights seemed to be fading. Then the dashboard lights quickly began to dim. Before I knew it, my nice little Mercedes was merely coasting down the highway in complete darkness.

Of course, those of you who have been driving for any length of time will recognize that it was an alternator that chose precisely that moment to go kaput and caused my dilemma. Although I generally do not believe in speaking of inanimate objects as if they possess animate qualities, I am absolutely convinced gadgets and gizmos will foil their human creators any chance they get. This is why I like my guns the way I like my cameras: point-and-shoot. The less technology to go wrong, the better.

So there I sat on the side of the road with no hazard lights. Absolutely nothing works when the alternator goes: no cell phone (they were just becoming popular, and there would not have been a signal out there anyway), no houses, no streetlights, no quickie marts, nothing! Just gale force winds that knocked the chill factor down to negative numbers and big, eighteen-wheeler trucks that blasted past me, creating more wind.

Now, I know what you are thinking: *Well, Suzanna, you should have been more prepared – Boy Scouts and all that.*

I was prepared! The very first thing I did after putting on my jacket was to place my revolver in a quickly accessible coat pocket. With absolute clarity, I realized without that little bit of insurance, I would be at the complete mercy of whoever eventually stopped to investigate my sidelined car.

Although I was able to act with confidence, I could not help but wonder at the dread another woman might have felt under the same circumstances. Can you imagine having to trust to chance that the vehicle stopping behind you contains a state trooper or a Good Samaritan rather than some deranged killer for whom the perfect opportunity had come along? Pondering that kind of vulnerability still gives me the willies.

My next step was to put out a ground flare. I got one lit and set it on the shoulder behind my car. I think it lasted about five minutes in that raging wind. After nearly an hour of hand waving a flashlight next to my raised hood, a truck driver braked and slowed to a stop some third of a mile or so ahead of me. Once I saw him get out and start jogging back my way, I got in my car, locked the door, and placed my hand on my pistol. That nice man spoke politely to me through the window I had lowered slightly, prior to losing all power.

I felt so rude, and my upbringing screamed at me to let this seeming savior in out of the frigid wind, or at least join him up in the cab of his rig. But I resisted the temptation, knowing any decent man would understand my caution and respect it. Although he seemed genuinely loathe to leave me on the side of the road, I convinced him I would be all right, without tipping my hand, and asked him to drive on ahead and call for roadside assistance at the first opportunity.

Not long after my Good Samaritan drove away in his truck, a New Mexico state trooper pulled over to check on the situation and quickly got a wrecker on its way. He said he had gone past me earlier, but saw no flashers, and assumed it was just an abandoned car. In his second passing, he had seen the truck driver leaving my window and decided the situation bore further investigation.

I had another stark realization in that forty-five minutes we waited for the tow truck to arrive. Chatting with the officer about how he had been anxious to get home to his family, I was suddenly aware of how vulnerable he was. As we sat warming ourselves in his patrol car, my still-frozen hands had remained in my coat pockets within easy reach of my gun. In our short talk, I came to know he felt strongly about the individual citizen's right to own and carry a firearm. He even taught some courses on it.

Just as I, although prepared and confident, was to some degree at the mercy of whoever stopped that night, he too, although prepared, confident, and highly trained, was at the mercy of whomever he stopped. That realization gave me a whole new respect and gratitude for the work those men and women do. Those folks truly put their lives on the line for us everyday, with every contact they make. I am not sure there is enough pay in the world for that.

My car was towed, and I eventually made it to my hotel. By the way, the officer's dispatcher confirmed the truck driver did indeed summon help for me. There are good people in the world.

There have been other times when I had my gun in my hand or in my pocket while checking out some odd circumstance or suspicious situation. The only time I can recall actually using it was several years ago, on the outskirts of Lampasas, Texas.

I kept a couple of horses at my sister and brother-in-law's house, and we were in the habit of exercising them in the afternoon and then finishing out the evening sitting on the porch, sipping martinis. About a third of the way through my drink, I noticed one of my sister's cats in a mesquite tree in a pasture bordering their yard. Not being a fan of felines, I made some derogatory remark about it hunting baby birds to eat.

About halfway through my glass, I saw the same fat, black cat on the ground and wisecracked about it switching gears to stalk baby rabbits. After a few more minutes of conversation in which we solved most of the world's problems, I suddenly heard a sound that, even though you have never heard it in real life before, makes you snap to instant attention with adrenaline rushing and muscles twitching in response to some primal instinct. For a very brief moment, my subconscious registered it as the distant chirping of cicadas.

Then I suddenly, and just instantly, knew! About a hundred feet away in the pasture, I saw the cat standing stock-still, staring at something directly to its right. Although I could not see it, I shouted, "Oh my God! There's a rattlesnake!"

My poor brother-in-law, Buddy, jumped out of his chair. His eyes searched the porch at our feet, and he shouted, "Where?!"

I replied, "No! Over there!" And I motioned in the direction of the frozen cat.

Buddy ran into the house to get his shotgun, while I made a mad dash to retrieve the Smith and Wesson from the purse in my car. As Erika and I approached the pasture, the rattling sound got significantly louder. At last we could see it. There, about twenty feet beyond the barbed wire fence and about eighteen inches from the side of the petrified tomcat, was the raised head of a small, western diamondback.

There was no easy way to get through the six-strand fence, and the light was beginning to fade. I spread my feet to shoulder width and brought my little snub nose .38 up with a two-handed grip. As I took a bead on the snake's head and began to slowly squeeze the trigger, my

The whole "new" family at Thanksgiving in 1984. Dad, me, Mom, Erika, Allan, and Allan's wife Kathy — and Tali the dog.

sister suddenly grabbed my arm and screamed, "Don't shoot my kitty!"

Frankly, it had not occurred to me. But I suppose it was a wise admonition on her part, considering my rather well-known, shall we say lack of fondness for well-fed domestic felines that still insist on torturing lesser animals until their deaths—too close to the behavior of some humans for my taste. Had it not been my sister's cat that was about to get nailed, I probably would have just sat back and let nature play it out.

But it was my sister's cat. So I re-aimed my little gun and pulled the trigger. In a flash, the tom flew one way, and the snake's head went the other! Erika cheered, and I was quite impressed with myself. Buddy jogged up and finished the rattler off with a shotgun blast moments later.

I am an incredibly mediocre shot. I do not practice enough and, to make matters worse, I have a nasty hand tremor that garnered quite a few jokes when I was in chiropractic college dissecting cadavers. "Good thing you're not considering becoming a brain surgeon."

There is only one reason I nailed that snake's head with a tiny .38 caliber Airweight from several yards away. Yep, you guessed it: the martini. Alcohol makes the type of tremor I have nearly disappear for a while, so my hands were temporarily, and uncharacteristically, steady as a rock. I do not make a habit of drinking and then handling loaded weapons, nor do I encourage it. It is just the way it happened that evening.

Erika and I spent the next little while skinning the snake, and occasionally the reptilian reflexes would cause its tail to come up and rattle. Even knowing its biting end was a hundred yards away, instinct still made us jump and yelp! After we skinned it, the two of us removed what backstrap we could get and fried it up in a pan with a little butter. With Buddy jokingly reading Bible verses about the serpent, we ate that little snake, and felt quite satisfied with ourselves. Heck, I even got a hatband out of it. But that's as close to hunting as I have ever gotten.

That was also my first experience with unloaded guns kept under lock and key. You see, Buddy would have been out there earlier with his much more appropriate shotgun, had it not been in a locked rifle cabinet, unloaded, with the shells in yet another locked drawer. Quick as he was, I am convinced the whole episode would have ended quite differently had the cat's fate been dependent on that safely stored shotgun.

There have been other times my little revolver has come in handy to put some hapless creature that had been struck by a car out of its misery. I seem to be adept at spotting injured animals other people assume are dead. I cannot bear the idea of anything lying in fear and pain for perhaps days waiting for death to come. Over the years, there have been seagulls, raccoons, jackrabbits, opossums, and more than a couple of deer either I or my wonderful husband have quickly put out of their misery. To me, death is one thing…suffering is an entirely different matter.

Then, on one particular day in 1984, some lunatic went into a MacDonald's in San Ysidro, California, and murdered twenty-one people. Men, women, children…it did not seem to matter to him. I can remember smugly and self-righteously thinking, "Well! That could never have happened if I had been there."

Sometimes life has a way of putting us in our place.

❖ ❖ ❖

CHAPTER 6
October 16th, 1991

It was an absolutely gorgeous day with clear, cool air and no hint of humidity…pretty typical for early Fall in the heart of Texas Hill Country. It reminded me very much of an autumn day in Albuquerque, where the sky seems surreally high, and the air tastes particularly good. In fact, several days earlier, Buddy and Erika hosted a birthday/anniversary get together for Mom and Dad.

For her birthday I gave Mom a plane ticket to Albuquerque scheduled to depart on the 23rd. The two of us were planning to catch part of the Arabian Horse National Championships I had not missed since 1977. On this fall day, I imagined I could already smell the piñon

My Arabian stallion "Shah" and me. Mom dragged me to the barn where we originally discovered this gem.

pine burning in the Albuquerque fireplaces. We were both eager to be on our way.

But that was a week away. On this day, I was busying myself treating patients at my clinic in Copperas Cove, secretly wishing I were anywhere outdoors instead. At the very least, I wished my office had an enormous sunroof and huge French doors. No such luck in the little strip center where I leased space, but not a bad idea for future construction!

The cute young man I had been dating was out of town, so I had no real plans for the day beyond taking care of my patients. Mid-morning, a good friend named Mark Kopenhafer called from his place of work. He was the number two manager at Luby's buffet-style chain restaurant in the nearby town of Killeen. As acting manager that day, he believed he could arrange for an actual sitdown meal of his own around lunchtime. So he called to ask if I could squeeze a few minutes out of what seemed to him my enviably long lunch break to grab a bite of lunch with him.

I understand most of the rest of the world does not take two-hour lunch breaks, but it is one of the perks of going to school six years; owing thousands in student loan debt; and taking on the responsibility of a new business with its own associated loans, dealing with employees, and hassling with taxes, insurance, and the like. So yes, I took a two- and sometimes three-hour lunch break. But I digress.

It just so happened on that particular Wednesday I actually did have a lot of little personal and business errands to run. I reluctantly declined his invitation for good food and conversation and went back to my morning patients.

My father was a semi-permanent fixture on the Copperas Cove Municipal Golf Course. No...make that a permanent fixture on the course. He was the first one there every morning and would often start the coffee pot for all who would follow. Even drizzle or snow would not keep him from playing the game that, as all true golfers would agree, borders on religion. I even threatened to have some golf cleats glued onto scuba flippers so he could continue to play in a deluge. The only thing that kept him from playing was a "Golf Course Is Closed Today" sign on the pro shop window.

He had many friends out there, and there were constant and typical golf jokes and silly pranks. One that sticks with me in particular concerns Dad and a much younger man with whom he rode and played the course frequently. He and Steve were great buddies. As I recall, the story went something like this:

About midway through the front nine — the back nine did not even exist then — there was a hole that required a pretty long drive off the men's tee to clear a small lake. Dad apparently routinely cleared it with room to spare. But Steve, normally a good golfer, managed to plunk one down into the middle of the lake. Undaunted, he went to the shared golf cart and got another ball.

Dad and Allan on their way to the golf course.

Dad posing with one of his golf trophies. He cleaned up at the "Lefties" tournaments.

Whack! Followed by sploosh! Another brand new Titleist was sent to a watery grave. Now any golfer knows you do not send good after bad. You pick up and move to the other side of the lake and take a stroke. But that is not what happened. While Dad was commiserating with him over the poor shots and the lost balls, Steve began giggling. He went back to the cart and got another brand new ball. Whack! Sploosh! My Dad said, "Are you nuts?" Steve's giggling turned into guffaws as he went back for another. One more time: Whack! Sploosh!

By now, Steve was doubled over with laughter, and tears were streaming from his eyes as he walked back to the cart for yet another ball. My poor father could stand it no longer. He caught his friend by the arm and said, "Steve! Those are brand new Titleists. They cost you too much to be wasting them for fun!"

Steve's response between howls? "Naw, they didn't cost me a thing. I've been getting them out of your bag!"

Such is golf humor.

On this particular day, my mother joined him on the course. Not a golfer herself, she simply loved the excuse to get outdoors and enjoy the beautiful weather. Mom would often ride in the cart with Dad and read, nature-watch, or chat with him about his book, of which she was chief editor. They must have had a particularly nice morning, because when they showed up at my clinic near lunchtime, they both had that happy glow that comes only from being generally content with life and communing with nature. For Dad that would mean the wood in the golf club and the grass on the tee box.

Although I was not expecting them that Wednesday morning, it certainly was not unusual for them to drop by. Dad was my bookkeeper, and Mom would often help review files and spot-check my staff's billing practices. She was a master at that and other organizational skills I lacked. Having two people available whom I could explicitly trust was a boon to my social life as well as my growing business.

I had finished with my morning patients and was in my office completing every doctor's least favorite duty, insurance paperwork, when my folks came in. Dad was in golf pants and shirt, and Mom was in jeans and a cute, feminine, cotton blouse with little blue flowers all over it. Silver and turquoise Indian feather earrings I had given her dangled from her lobes. Dad said he had to get one thing or another done to his pickup truck at an auto shop over in Killeen, and they thought they would grab some lunch across the highway at the Luby's cafeteria. Would I like to join them?

I explained, as I had a short while earlier to Mark, I had too many errands to run that day, and I was just planning on grabbing a quick bite at home. But they persisted, and even volunteered to do some of those chores for me later that afternoon. So as my stomach growled and my willpower faded, I soon capitulated.

Dad drove his truck, and Mom joined me in my car for the twelve minutes or so it took to get from Copperas Cove to Killeen. On the way, Mom and I covered several topics. We spoke of the fun we all had on the previous weekend when we celebrated both their October 3rd wedding anniversary and her October 1st birthday at my sister's house, not far from where we were driving in Killeen.

Erika and her husband, Buddy Boylan, had us all over frequently. We would play cards or some other game, while Buddy would typically cook something that used to breathe — meat, lots and lots of meat — on his beloved propane grill and serve us Buddy-style vodka martinis, Manhattans, or cosmopolitans. We spent that evening getting pleasantly tipsy, while playing a silly game of croquet we set up in the roughs around the Boylan's home. I had a date with me. Greg was younger than I, which, in my mind at the time, made him ineligible for a serious relationship. Even worse, he was in the Army (I had my career to consider), and he had been a patient (all right, I guess the past tense on this one made it OK). On the other hand, he was tall, lean, and hunky; worked in military intelligence (German interrogator, no less); and was just a nice guy. Did I mention he was tall, lean, and hunky? Mom thought he had "bedroom eyes." Mom!

During our drive to the cafeteria, we also talked about plans for their 50th wedding anniversary. The possibilities were limited only by our imaginations and money. We knew it would be fun. Big party, little party….I was secretly hoping my brother and I could put enough money aside to send them to Hawaii. What a great surprise that would be!

We followed Dad up to the point where he dropped off his truck and waited for him as arrangements were made to have the necessary work done. He came out, jumped in the back seat of my car, and we made the short trip beneath the underpass and to the restaurant.

Mom and Dad in the late eighties.

I liked going there. Not only did my buddy Mark work there, but they also had great food! It was the only place in town where you could load up on good veggies and count on the desserts to be varied and scrumptious. The parking lot was packed, but we found a space off to the left side of the building where I could fit my car.

Luby's was largely square with a front-centered entrance and a covered, drive-through drop-off area. Floor-to-ceiling windows surrounded the entire right side of the building that held the dining area. The kitchen and buffet line were to the left of the entrance.

We walked in, only to find the inside of the restaurant was just as busy as the parking lot. It was Boss's Day—yet another ridiculous manufactured "Day" to provide greeting card companies with a bigger bottom line—and the day after payday, so everyone in the business community was out lunching at one or another of our few eating establishments. We got in the long queue with everyone else, certain it would move as quickly as it always did. I can recall thinking Mom looked especially cute in her springy blouse and earrings.

When we got up to the buffet, we moved through quickly. I got the chicken tetrazzini, coconut cream pie, and iced tea. Mark spotted us and offered to join us at our table. The seating area was as full of patrons as every-where else, and we had to forego our usual spot near the front entrance for an empty table against the window on the right side of the cafeteria. I chose a seat across from my parents, facing the front windows, with most of the other diners to my right and behind me. Mark sat on my left.

I remember a young couple, acquaintances of mine, seated behind me, and a couple of tables to their right were some chiropractors from whom I had purchased my clinic: the patriarch and his wife, their son and daughter-in-law, and their tiny, new baby granddaughter asleep in a carrier next to them.

The four of us enjoyed a leisurely meal cussing and discussing life and politics — is there a difference? — and had moved on to coffee and dessert, when Mark got pulled away temporarily to deal with some mini-crisis in the kitchen.

That is when it began.

Without warning, a pickup truck seemed to explode through one of the front windows where we usu-ally sat, sending shards of glass everywhere and top-pling tables and people alike. It jerked to a halt as the driver threw it into park about fifteen feet to my right. The vehicle was completely inside the building and still gyrating up and down on its shock absorbers from the suddenness of its stop. As I sat temporarily immobilized, I remember thinking what a shame the accident hap-pened: all of those people injured — I did not know how badly — and such a pretty, new truck all dented up. It was

a terrible shame, all the way around. As the initial surprise wore off, I began to rise from my seat to go to the
aid of the folks sprawled across the floor from the impact.

Suddenly, I heard a gunshot. Although we recognized it
as gunfire, it was odd how the acoustics of the dining area
reduced it to a mere "popping" noise. Just like the sound
the rattlesnake makes, it commanded full and immediate
attention. My father and I instantly dropped to the floor
and turned the table onto its side in front of us, to serve as
our only shield. Mom got down behind us, between Dad
and the window.

Several more shots followed. It occurred to me this was
no accident: this was a robbery! I trained my ears onto the
bad guy, certain he would say something like, "Everybody
put your wallets on the table!" But instead, he began shooting down the buffet line opposite us as he stepped out of
his truck. Then I thought, "This is a hit." After all, it was
Boss's Day, and I have watched far too much TV—maybe
someone important was in here.

But he kept shooting. I peeked over the top of our
upturned table. He was not spraying bullets. I was
shocked to see he was simply walking from one person
to the next, taking aim, and pulling the trigger. In total,
it took me about forty-five seconds to figure out this guy
was just going to walk around and execute people. Forty-
five seconds is an eternity.

Back then things like this were not happening routinely, so it certainly was not the first thing that came to
my mind. There was a moment I was sure some police
officer—they always ate there—would take him out. But
he seemed to have no opposition of any kind as he continued his bloody march. Forty-five seconds before I knew
my and my parents' lives were in grave danger. Forty-five
seconds…and about eight innocent people shot dead.

At that point, the gunman was rounding the front of
his vehicle, his right shoulder toward me, when it dawned
on me, "I've got him!" I reached for my purse that lay

on the floor next to the chicken tetrazzini. I had a perfect place to prop my hand to help stabilize my little revolver on the upturned table in front of us. Everyone else in the restaurant was down, he was up, perhaps fifteen feet from me, and I have hit much smaller targets at much greater distances.

Then it occurred to me with sudden and utter clarity that, just a few months earlier, I had made the stupidest decision of my life: my gun was not in my purse any longer! I had done what many people do: I had rationalized that the chance of my needing it was slim, and the chance of getting caught with it somewhat higher. I had figured, "Oh, what are the odds I'll need this thing in a crowded place in the middle of the day? If I ever need it, it's going to be if my car breaks down on one of these dark Texas roads, out in the middle of nowhere." I did not want to risk getting caught with it somewhere and potentially losing my license to practice chiropractic. After all, that was my livelihood we were talking about.

So there it was, tucked neatly behind the passenger seat of my car, a hundred yards away, completely useless to me.

Jarred back to the very stark reality of being completely defenseless, I began looking for other potential weapons: there was my purse—I sarcastically thought I could throw it at him knowing it was heavy enough to do damage. There was the standard butter knife, not even sharp enough to cut open a dinner roll. Then there were saltshakers and other table items I quickly concluded were worthless against an enemy with, not only one, but two handguns. My mind began to race. I had often heard how time would slow down in life-and-death situations, but I was still operating in real time—time that was growing shorter with each step he took in our direction.

You would think the place would have been all panic and pandemonium. But in truth, it was oddly quiet and still, except for the popping sound of the gun and an occasional short scream or quick directive like, "Get down!" I was later told the gunman shouted a few slurs and epithets, but I was never aware of them. Nor do I care what he said.

No Way Out

We were basically in a corner with no way out, and he was coming down the aisle directly toward us. I can't begin to get across to you what it's like to sit there and wait for it to be your turn. I get very angry even now just thinking about it. Can you imagine not being able to fight back? I began plotting some last act of defiance. The old cartoon of a hawk swooping down on a tiny mouse that had its middle finger extended came to mind.

Then my father grabbed my attention. Crouching to my left, he began saying, "I've got to do something. I've got to do something. He's going to kill everyone in here." Dad began to make a move in the gunman's direction. I could see him searching for the right moment. I grabbed him by the shirt collar and tried to hold him down, saying, "Yeah, and if you go out there, he'll shoot you too!"

But, when Dad saw what he thought was a chance, and just before the bad guy had reached my chiropractic friends' table, he stood up and lunged toward the man. He covered half the distance in a moment. But the gunman had complete control of the entire restaurant. He saw my father coming, and he simply turned, raised his pistol, and fired.

My father went down in the aisle maybe seven or eight feet from me. He was alive, and still conscious, but the wound to his chest was horrific. I knew he would die, and as terrible as it sounds, I basically wrote him off. I turned my thoughts toward my mother's and my own survival.

With my father's body blocking the aisle, the murderer changed directions slightly. Instead of continuing straight toward us, he angled off to my left. It amazes me what stupid little thoughts our gray matter can unleash at times. As he was standing six feet or so from me, with his arm extended in the firing pose, I remember really looking at him for the first time. He was tall and well-built, good-looking in jeans, polo shirt, and a cap. I remember thinking, "What could be so wrong in this guy's life? Thirty-something, nice-looking, new truck: I'd have gone out with him."

The mind is a funny thing.

I was brought sharply back to reality when someone broke out a window way at the back of the dining area in the smoking section. When I heard the glass shatter, I thought, "Oh no! Here comes another one!" I was still searching my mind for some logical explanation for what was happening, when there was none. I briefly entertained the idea of more than one terrorist attacking us because of our proximity to Fort Hood. But as I looked toward the sound, fully expecting to see another armed nutcase, I saw instead an accidental hero at work.

An Escape Route

I later learned the young man, who had been enjoying his lunch hour like the rest of us, had repeatedly attempted to kick through one of the floor-to-ceiling windows. After several failed attempts, he actually stood up and launched his own large frame through the glass. In doing so, he opened up a huge avenue of escape for people in that section of the restaurant. Patrons were pouring out the big opening and onto the grassy area immediately behind the cafeteria.

But no one was making a move from my non-smoking area — no doubt like me, afraid to move and call attention to themselves while in such close proximity to the killer. I peeked up over the top of the table and waited several more seconds. When the gunman was several yards away and by the back of his pickup, I decided to make my move. I stood up and turned toward my mother, who was semi-crouched on the floor up against the side window. I realized I was completely exposed at that moment and, since I had my back to the shooter, I did not know if he was looking at me or not. Every time I heard his gunfire, I expected to feel the impact of the bullet against my back that would send me lurching forward.

I vividly recalled from my youthful incident how I did not feel immediate pain from the bullet, just incredible impact. I imagined how much worse the impact from a 9 mm would be. I reached down, grabbed my mother by the shirt collar, and said, "Come on, come on! We've got to run! We've got to get out of here!" She did not speak, but made a few breathy, startled sounds as she shifted forward as if to rise and follow me.

Then my feet grew wings. It is amazing how fast one can move in high heels. I ran to the huge opening in the

*Police examining the window at the back of the restaurant
broken by one of the patrons to provide
an escape route from the gunfire inside.
(Todd Drumwright/Killeen Daily Herald)*

A look through the back window broken by one
of the patrons to escape the gunfire inside.
(Lee Schexnaider/Killeen Daily Herald)

window at the back of the restaurant, where I had seen so many people get out a few minutes earlier. As I neared it, I imagined the shots I continued to hear were now aimed in our direction as he began to lose control of his audience.

A handful of people were still escaping through the makeshift exit, and as I stumbled over one—Was she injured? Why didn't I stop to help her?—my loss of balance and momentum sent me over the eight-inch-high brick ledge and onto my hands and knees in the grass and broken glass behind the building.

It was there panic set in. Maybe it was the sheer act of running that disengaged my mind and set the adrenalin coursing through me. I really don't know. I had lost one shoe in the act of stumbling and quickly kicked off the other so I could make a faster get away. My heart was racing, and I was thinking what it would be like for my boyfriend and others to hear of my death.

I scrambled to my bare feet and had continued another few yards from the building, when Mark burst through a rear exit door several yards away from the busted out window. We both said, "Thank God you're OK," and I continued with, "but Dad was hit, and it's bad!"

Where Was Mom?

I turned to say something to my mom and only then realized she had not followed me out. Mark and I quickly looked in the direction of the table where we had been enjoying each other's company only minutes before. We could not make out detail with the relative darkness of the building interior and the backlighting from the windows at the front of building. We were not sure where the gunman was or if he was moving in our direction. Nor could we see my mother.

Mark pointed across the street to indicate the direction many of the patrons had already fled, and said, "You run to those apartments and get help! I've got to go back in and make sure all my kitchen help can get out!" Then, he turned and reentered his workplace through a delivery door. It remains one of the outright gutsiest and bravest acts I have ever witnessed.

I sprinted across the small field, crossed the street, and entered the courtyard of an already chaotic apartment complex. I saw a few people looking lost and milling about. Almost immediately, a young man in a second story apartment hollered at me through his open window and motioned to me to come on up. I could see he had a phone to his ear explaining to a 9-1-1 operator what was happening.

I did not wait for a second invitation. I bolted up the stairs, still imagining the bad guy may be hot on my heels. The startled-looking fellow opened the door for me, still on the phone, and I recall asking, "Do you have a gun?! Do you have a gun?!" as I burst into his apartment. He was obviously surprised by the question, but replied he did not have one. He offered me a wet washcloth to clean my wounds instead. I had not realized it, but I had gotten quite a few cuts on my arms and feet when I fell into the broken glass. I still feel guilty about the mess I must have left in his apartment.

When he hung up, I asked if I could make a few calls. I knew my sister was teaching at an elementary school not too many miles from there, but did not know the number, so I chanced a call to her home. By some good fortune, I got her husband Buddy, quickly told him what had happened, and asked him to go pick up Erika. Then I called my brother's house, and an answering machine clicked on. I quickly relayed the story and told them to head this way. My third and final call was to my clinic. I knew they would soon get word of the shootings, and I wanted to let them know I was OK. I also wanted them to be able to cancel the afternoon's appointments and field any phone calls they might get from my siblings.

I thanked the young man for his help and the use of his telephone, and apologized for the bloody washcloth.

The front of the restaurant after the incident.
(Killeen Daily Herald)

Police watch outside the restaurant as ambulance crews
remove victims from the scene. The window to the right
is where the truck crashed into the building.
(Lee Schexnaider/Killeen Daily Herald)

Then, I hurried downstairs to a small breezeway where a
few people had gathered. To my horror and amazement,
I could still hear shots being fired. There was a policeman
nearby behind the open door of his cruiser, and I recognized him as a patient. I yelled to him, but he gave me a
hand signal to stay put.

Within another minute or two, the gunfire ceased and
everything became silent momentarily. Joe, the policeman,
was talking into his radio as he walked over to me. He
said it was all over, though he did not know details. He
motioned to me to follow him, and for a second I hesitated. I was not at all crazy about getting back out in the
open again, not until I was convinced that maniac was
dead or handcuffed in the back of a squad car.

As the officer escorted me toward the back of the
restaurant, I filled him in on what had happened. I saw
ambulances and helicopters already descending upon the
scene. When we got to the area where I had fallen through
the busted out window, I spotted my shoes. Although we
were only a few yards from them, Joe would not let me

retrieve them. He said something about the investigation and kept me moving forward. Then his radio crackled with the news the gunman was dead. No further information was given.

As we rounded the side of the building and started down the front sidewalk, the activity level increased dramatically. Our walk led us past the jagged hole in the plate glass where, just a few feet inside the restaurant, the backend of the wrecked truck looked so out of place. Just beyond, lay the covered drive-through in front of what was the normal patrons' entrance. There were cops and emergency personnel everywhere, and the media had already begun its feeding frenzy.

Dad Was Dead

It was then that I saw him. My father was lying on a stretcher placed on the ground perhaps a dozen feet from me. I knew in an instant he was dead. His eyes were open and had that flat, empty stare that could never be

*Officers walk around in the restaurant near
the window where the truck crashed through.
(Lee Schexnaider/Killeen Daily Herald)*

mistaken for mere loss of consciousness. His shirt was covered in blood. There was a small, dark river coming from somewhere beneath his body, and it formed a pool in a little depression in the pavement near his side. The color of his skin reflected the blood loss. I instantly moved in his direction and blurted out, "Oh, Dad...."

Joe stepped in front of me with his hands up as if to block my way and said something like, "Take it easy. Take it easy. It's too late for him now."

I immediately felt guilty for not having hurried back to this spot. If I had been a little quicker in getting back around the building to where he lay, could I have held his hand as he died? I mentally kicked myself. Hard.

I quickly asked Joe if I could enter the restaurant to look for my mother. He told me it was already cordoned off, and even my purse would remain inside for now. I looked him in the eye and, suddenly, my brain shifted into a different gear. Like Dad, I had to do something. I assured him I was in control of myself, and asked him twice, "What can I do to help? What can I do?" As I spoke, out of the corner of my eye, I saw a paramedic pull a sheet up over my father's body and face.

Joe looked around at the overwhelming number of people who had arrived to help. There were law enforcement personnel of every type, emergency medical technicians, paramedics, Army emergency personnel sent from nearby Fort Hood, helicopters from the base as well as nearby hospitals, TV news crews, newspaper photographers, and any number of passersby who thought they could lend a hand. The parking lot had rapidly become a sea of people. Joe made a few inquiries, but determined the other surviving patrons and employees had been sent across the neighboring bank parking lot to the Sheraton Hotel beyond, where a command post of sorts was being set up.

At that moment, my sister and her husband rushed up to me from out of the mass of people and activity. She caught me by the arm and asked simply, "Dad?"

I looked at her and said just as simply, "He's gone."

Erika crumpled onto the curb with her head in her hands and wailed. Then she was up and in my arms as I hugged and tried to soothe her. The whole scenario lasted only seconds before she regained control, but that was the moment some newspaper photographer snapped our picture.

She pushed me back and asked, "What about Mom?"

I said, "I don't know, but I don't think it's good. They won't let me back in there to check, and I didn't see her out here. She may have been wounded and taken to a hospital. But Erika, this guy wasn't shooting to wound."

My sister spotted a man on a stretcher being loaded onto an ambulance. Something about the scene made her think it was the killer. She dove toward him, but her husband stopped her. I do believe had it actually been the gunman and had my sister been allowed to reach him, there would have been nothing left for a trial.

My cop friend suggested perhaps Mom had already gone to the Sheraton and was waiting for us there. So the three of us set out across the parking lot. Upon arriving in the lobby of the hotel, we were directed into a large room they often used for banquets. From there, they seemed to be taking people in small groups to individual rooms. Most had already been moved.

I recognized a restaurant employee and sat at her table while Erika and Buddy tried to find out what was going on. While talking to the young woman, I began hyperventilating for the first and, I hope, the only time in my life. I realized what I was doing and had to make a conscious effort to get control of my breathing. Within a minute or two—what seemed like an eternity—my breathing became normal again.

My brother-in-law soon returned, and I followed him to one of several rooms the hotel had graciously opened up to us on the ground floor. The door was propped open, and I walked in to find my sister already seated at the far end of the room. For quite a while, many strangers came and went. The American Red Cross and others had put out a call for psychologists and counselors and any people trained in trauma-care therapy, and they descended on the hotel within less than an hour.

Mark Maintained Control

We had been there for thirty or forty minutes, with several well-meaning people entering and exiting the room, when the familiar face of my friend, Mark, entered the room. But his usual bright expression was ashen. He cried, "Suzy, your mother's dead! I'm so sorry! I'm so sorry!" He cried in my arms, as if he had somehow been responsible. I reassured him we were OK, and I told him how grateful I was that he was alive.

Mark explained how, after he had reentered the building to make sure his workers could escape, he went to his office to call 9-1-1. Before he could complete the call, the shooting sounded closer, so he bolted to an exit for the second time. After the cops arrived, and the shootout had ceased, he convinced them he had to reenter the building one last time to make sure ovens were turned off and avert a fire. He actually had the wherewithal to lock up the cash drawer and make a call to the main office in San Antonio, as well. Somehow they had already been alerted, and one of the head honchos was on his way and asked Mark questions from his car phone.

I can only imagine what it must have been like to be on the other end of that line as, according to Mark, the conversation went something like this: "Mr. (Head Honcho), I understand you've already been told there has been a shooting here."

"Yes, I'm on my way. Do you have everything locked up?"

"Yes."

"Do you think we can re-open by dinnertime?"

Long pause. "Uh, sir…I'm at the serving line and can't even see the rest of the cafeteria, but I can count eight bodies from here."

Silence. "Oh my God; I had no idea. I'll be there as quickly as I can."

Mark convinced the cops a second time he had to enter the main dining area for some made-up reason. He said he found Mom there, several feet from our table, with her face already covered with a napkin by a paramedic who had swept through the room on an initial triage. Mark did not look more closely; he did not have to. He recognized her pretty cotton blouse with the little blue flowers.

I am still amazed at what he put himself through for my family and so many others.

When he left the room, I attempted to call my sister-in-law, Kathy, at her home once again, but got no answer. I just

Mark Kopenhafer, my friend and the manager of the Killeen Luby's on that fateful day.

could not bring myself to call my brother Allan at his own chiropractic clinic in a distant town. So, in desperation, I telephoned his best friend's clinic. It was someone with whom we had both gone to college and I knew I could count on. When Kevin got on the line, I briefly explained to him what had happened and begged him to go to my brother's clinic and break the news. He agreed without hesitation.

As I hung up the phone, I suddenly became aware of the blood I was tracking all over the hotel carpet. My bare feet had been sliced to ribbons on the broken glass. I went to the restroom to inspect the damage, hiked myself up onto the counter and began flushing out a few of the particularly nasty cuts in the sink.

I noticed an ugly rip in the dress I had on. It was one of my favorites Mom had made for me. Of course, with the door propped open and hotel bathrooms being situated as they are, everyone was still able to come and go, hold conversations with us, and inquire about the miniscule wounds I was washing. Several people had asked if I needed medical attention for the cuts on my feet, arms, and hands, but I insisted all I needed were some Band-Aids.

There was one particularly dogged young Army therapist who kept insisting I was "…gonna' blow. If not now, then six months from now." She tried to convince Erika and Buddy I was "too calm" and "must be in shock," and she was adamant that I go to the hospital. I continued to refuse, but did my best to reassure her, adding, "Look, I can't say I won't blow a gasket six months from now, but right this minute, I'm OK."

My Support Structure

She switched tactics and asked me questions about my support structure. I waved my hand toward Buddy and Erika and told her, with a few out-of-town exceptions, she was looking at it. When I mentioned the young military guy I was dating, she perked up and asked specifics. I explained to her what I was sure she already knew: since Greg and I were not married or engaged, and since he was on a training mission at some camp near San Antonio, there was no way the Army was going to let him come support me. But thanks for asking.

She renewed her argument that I should go to a hospital and be checked out. Just then, a friend and business associate—a radiologist from a nearby hospital—walked by my open door. I called out to him, determined I was not going to ride anywhere in an ambulance when my wounds were far from life threatening. When he entered our room, I introduced him to the zealous therapist in battle dress uniform. In her presence, I asked if he was headed back to the hospital, and then asked if I could ride with him and be checked out. He was kind enough to say, "Of course!" So the soldier/therapist was finally appeased.

The short ride to the hospital provided a brief respite from the flurry of activity and whirlwind of emotions that surrounded me at the hotel. Before I left, my brother-in-law said he would be by the hospital to pick me up as quickly as possible. Once there, I was quickly x-rayed and examined to make sure no glass was imbedded in any of my wounds. A doctor determined some butterfly bandages and glue would suffice in place of stitches on my feet and arm.

The hospital staff, some of whom I knew, were amazingly kind. It must have been very difficult for them to know what to say or do for patients in that situation. But, they managed the crisis in a way that was soothing, as well as helpful, to those of us in their care. As I lay on the examining table awaiting the x-ray results, they offered up their phone so I could notify anyone else I felt compelled to reach.

With their permission, I placed an expensive call to an old boyfriend, who had also been a family friend for about seven years and was working in the United Arab

Emirates. I suspected the incident would be all over CNN, and I did not think he should find out about it that way. After giving him the news, I told him not to come, as I knew how expensive a trip back to the States would be. I was OK, and the only thing left to do for my parents…was a funeral.

When the x-ray results arrived, and I was deemed well enough to be released, I got up and met Buddy out in the hall. The doctor who examined me was seated near him, jotting down some notes. He looked up at me momentarily and hesitated, seemingly at a loss for words. Then he asked, "Would you like something to help you sleep tonight?"

I smiled, put my arm around Buddy's shoulder, and said, "My brother-in-law makes the best vodka martinis in town. I figure two of those should do the trick! Thanks anyway." Then Buddy, my sister, and I headed out to their car.

CHAPTER 7
First Interviews

Bad news travels fast.

I am not too sure about the chronology of the rest of the day's events. But I know it was not long after arriving at Buddy and Erika's house that people started calling and showing up. Apparently, the phone lines leading into and out of Killeen were jammed with callers, either checking on some loved one, or letting someone know they were all right. In those days, it was still a rarity for someone to have a cellular phone in their pocket or purse. At some point, I think Buddy talked to either Allan or Kathy on a landline and knew they were on their way. By late afternoon, they had arrived.

I went outside to meet them as they rolled to a stop. Allan and Kathy had their daughters Katie, 7, Melissa, 4, and Christie, 1, with them. I went to Allan as he got out of their car and hugged him as he cried. He said he wanted so badly to be able to play one more round of golf with Dad, it just made him ache. It had been days since he talked to our folks, but he remembered the last call ended with "I love you." Thank God for that.

A little later he explained to all of us how he had gotten word of the tragedy.

Regardless of one's religion, or lack thereof, few people would argue that there exists some cosmic, unexplainable connection among all living things, and it is particularly powerful where love exists. My brother experienced that unfathomable link at about twelve fifteen that day, when for no apparent reason, he glanced down at his watch while treating a patient and was momentarily stopped in his tracks with a feeling of dread. He did what most of us would do: shook it off and continued to work.

About an hour later, he saw his friend Kevin walking up to the clinic entrance. As common an occurrence as that was, he knew this time was different. His first thoughts were of me. He felt certain something had happened to his sister Suzy. Kevin, bless his heart, assured him of my safety, but imparted what information he had about Mom and Dad as quickly and kindly as possible.

Kathy, meanwhile, had arrived home and gotten my message on their answering machine. She said she could clearly hear gunfire repeating in the background, and she could not bear to have Allan hear it. So she quickly erased my message and headed for his clinic.

Erika described how she had been busily teaching her first-grade class, when she was asked to come to the principal's office. She was told very briefly that her husband, Buddy, had called and was on his way to pick her up. There had been a shooting at a restaurant and her father had been involved. She dropped her face to her hands and, with overwhelming certainty, stated her father had been shot in the head. That was not exactly correct, for he had been struck in the chest. Some people would pass this kind of statement off to chance, but she did not know her mother and many others had indeed also been involved, and most had been shot in the head.

As the evening wore on, others arrived at Erika's house. There were Allan's in-laws, Mark and Claudette Bender, Buddy's pastor, as well as a couple of other folks from their church, a few of Erika's close friends from school, and a neighbor or two. It got quite busy very quickly, and I relocated with my martini to the porch.

Evening began to settle in, and the air took on a slight chill, but it was still a remarkably beautiful autumn twilight. It is funny how, when something awful has happened to you, you feel the rest of the universe should reflect that. The sky should turn gloomy, the leaves on the sumacs should not be such an impossible shade of red, and there certainly should not be any comedians doing stand-up routines on television. But the world somehow keeps revolving on its axis, the wind keeps blowing, and lives immediately begin moving on.

I sat on the porch, sipping my vodka and trying to grasp why that mockingbird was still singing, when a lady I did not know came out of the house and stood beside me. She was silent for several moments, then put her hands on her hips and said, "Well." There was a pause as she inhaled and exhaled rather loudly, never took her eyes off the horizon and continued, "Damn."

I looked up at her from the picnic table where I sat and suddenly — much to her surprise, I think — began to laugh. Here she was, this complete stranger to me, and she had summed it all up in a way that left nothing to doubt. It struck me as even more comprehensive than that old bumper sticker: "S--t happens."

"Damn." Yep, that pretty much covers it.

Sometime later that night, while still at my sister's house, I received a call. To my amazement, it was Greg phoning from the Army training facility just outside of San Antonio. His superiors had received word of the incident, in large part due to that wonderful female soldier who was so intent on my going to the hospital and persistent in her line of questioning about my support structure. Although it certainly was against protocol, given our merely-dating status, they had given him the OK to leave camp in the morning to be with me for as long as necessary. Perhaps they recognized the whole, horrible incident was against protocol.

I will be forever grateful to those involved with getting my future husband home to me.

I cannot recall exactly when Kathy Washer arrived from her home in Bandera, Texas. I believe Kevin called her and filled her in with as much as he knew. Allan, Kevin, Kathy, and I had all gone to chiropractic college together and had remained good friends. To my knowledge, she did not call us first; she did not have to. She just showed up, a very welcome shoulder to cry on. I believe she is the reason the rest of my family allowed me to return to my own home and bed that night. They knew she would be there to help me in any way necessary until we all got back together at the Boylan home on the following day. I was glad to have her there.

I had spent many weekends in Bandera with Kathy Washer, dancing at the Cabaret with all the local cowboys and just getting out of my small town, where I did not feel I could let my hair down and have fun. After all, I had to maintain a respectable, doctor-like reputation. Not that we would get that wild, but I figured I could avoid a lot of rumors by doing most of my playing in a town a hundred and eighty miles away from my clinic. Greg had begun to go there with me, which just added to the enjoyment.

I had a lot of nightmares that night. There is a big surprise, huh? Each time I closed my eyes, the horrible events of the day would repeat themselves. Most of the time, I was not fully or even nearly asleep when the visions would recur. I could not help constantly reliving, rehashing, and what-ifing the events of the day to the point of exhaustion. What if I had had my gun? What if I had kept Dad from rushing the guy? What if I had persevered a few extra moments and made certain my mother had gotten on her feet and followed me out? This was the one that haunted me the most. I felt I had failed her. And myself.

I have since known many people who have been given various prescription medications to help them get through those first few days and nights after a tragedy. Several times I second-guessed my decision not to accept the emergency room doctor's offer. But in hindsight, I believe people who are doped-up through that initial shock period really miss a part of the normal process the brain and heart must go through in order to heal. In clinics such as mine, where we deal with physical trauma, we know taking certain anti-inflammatories in the first few days following a sprain or strain causes the pain initially to be dulled, but the healing stage can be prolonged or even incomplete. Neither option is pleasant, but I chose to meet the days to come without the benefit of a drug-induced haze.

The Second Day

When morning on the second day finally arrived, Kathy and I drove back to Buddy and Erika's house. It had become the unofficial gathering place. Word had already been passed around that the bodies had been taken to a morgue, and since there was a crime involved, autopsies would have to be performed. I was still without my purse and my car, and the police told us all the personal effects and vehicles would be released later that day. We also received a phone call from the crime victims unit informing us of a counselor who would be available to my siblings and me at the Sheraton. So we made a loose appointment for that afternoon.

The phone calls from the press began bright and early, as well. By noon, hundreds of media units from this country and any other country with a modicum of press began swarming all over the restaurant parking lot and surrounding areas. We quickly discovered the snapshot taken of Erika and me on the day before had been immortalized on the front page of one of the big newspapers with an incorrect caption. It read something like, "Dr. Suzanna Gratia comforts an unidentified victim of the mass shooting that occurred at a Luby's cafeteria in Killeen, Texas."

We also became aware the event had the dubious honor of being the largest mass shooting ever to occur in the United States. Whether or not to talk to the press rapidly became a hot topic in the Boylan's living room that morning. Our initial inclination was to remain silent. But with further discussion, we determined the press was going to run with something. That was a given. How could we be angry with them for printing or saying the wrong thing if no one told them the right thing? That front-page picture with the incorrect caption was the perfect example. With that revelation, the decision was made.

I believe the first telephone interview I did was with a United Press International (UPI) reporter over the phone. Regardless of what terrible stories you may have heard about the abhorrent behavior of media personnel at such times, I was always dealt with in a very kind, polite, and apologetic manner. Reporters are, in fact, just people. I did my best to repeat the story of what happened to an Associated Press (AP) writer also, always including the frustration I felt at not having my gun in my purse. Each time, the writer could not help but ask the required, "How does that make you feel?" question. Each time, my answer was met with some surprise.

I said, "I'm not angry at the guy who did it. We're not talking about a career criminal. We're talking about some-one who went nuts. That's like being angry at a rabid dog. You might have to kill it, but you're not angry at it. But, I'll tell you what, I'm mad as hell at my legislators for legislat-ing me out of the right to protect myself and my family."

I do not think that was the answer they were expecting.

The word got around very quickly that someone at our phone number was willing to do interviews, and the phone rang continuously. After just a few, I found myself wrung out. Kathy Washer graciously began fielding the calls and let everyone else know they could get the story off the wire. She also acted as a call screener so friends and family could still get through.

Allan, Erika, and I did go to the Sheraton for a session with a well-intentioned and clearly overwhelmed coun-selor. I do not think it really helped any of us, but then again, it did not hurt either. I think some of the best counseling we received was given to each other on the drive to and from the hotel. We talked about how the whole scenario stunk. The three of us, suddenly, were orphans. Considering our ages, that may seem to be a ridiculous assessment. But the day before, we had had involved, caring parents whom we had every reason to believe would be around for many years to come.

On the other hand, there was a bright side: my brother and I, in particular, had seen many older couples in our practices where one would be diagnosed with some dreaded terminal disease, typically cancer. While the spouse helplessly looked on, the one with the illness would slowly wither away until they were bedridden and often in a great deal of uncontrolled pain. When death would eventually come, the surviving spouse's grief was temporarily mixed with relief. But so often, especially if they had been married for many decades, the remaining spouse would pass away within six months of the first. It is a phenomenon the medical community is well aware of.

In our case, yes, it was before their time. Yes, it was the result of a violent act. But, they also died relatively quickly… and together. We found some comfort in that.

Greg arrived later that evening. As we stood outside and he put his arms around me, my heart suddenly let go, and I wept for what seemed like an eternity. Kathy Washer had come out of the house briefly, but returned to inform everyone inside that "the dam finally broke."

❖ ❖ ❖

CHAPTER 8
Mom's Last Moments

Eventually, burial arrangements had to be made. In an act of kindness, while Allan, Erika, and I sat in the funeral home's office, a platter of food was delivered to us from my local bank. We were so grateful to them. It is amazing how one can forget to eat under those circumstances. The poor funeral director, who along with his wife was a patient of mine, did not quite seem to know how to handle our occasional attempts at humor.

Both Allan and I would like to have moved forward with cremation, because we were both uncomfortable with the whole six-feet-under thing. However, Dad had mentioned more than once he did not like the idea of cremation. I think he actually said he wasn't "too hot on it." Erika was not at all happy with the idea of purchasing simple, wooden coffins, i.e., pine boxes, for the burial. So we opted for a pair of step-up-from-the-pine-box coffins; the kind that are hermetically sealed for twenty-odd years.

I really did not see the point: you know, dust to dust and all that sort of thing. How would we get our money back if the seals failed or leaked in ten years? More importantly, how would we know? But we wanted Erika to be comfortable with the decision, so we quickly reached a compromise.

Where to bury them was an easy decision to make. Since Dad was a veteran, we could have him and Mom interred together at Fort Sam Houston Cemetery in San Antonio.

Amazingly, considering my age at the time, I had never even been to any funeral, much less that of someone near and dear to me. I had to learn quickly. A memorial was held in Copperas Cove's funeral chapel a couple of days later, and I can recall standing in my closet hours before its start, staring at my clothes. I knew black was the traditional mourning garb. But perhaps I should have been born into some other culture, because I felt certain we were supposed to be celebrating their lives. I thought one of the many pretty outfits my mom had made for me would be a far more meaningful choice.

The memorial ended up being standing room only, with closed, flag-draped caskets in the foreground. I wore a colorful skirt and vest Mom had sewn. Neither my parents nor I regularly attended a church at that time, so Buddy supplied a pastor from a church he frequented. Frankly, the whole ceremony stunk. There were no eulogies or speeches, just the pastor's impersonal rhetoric and a few prayers.

Now that I have been to several memorials and know how they should be conducted, I am regretful. I discovered later there were so many friends who wanted to speak but never got the opportunity to share their stories and recollections. I know the ceremony did not provide the closure intended.

My brother, boyfriend, and a few friends and patients spent the next day cleaning out Mom and Dad's apartment in Copperas Cove. I am forever grateful to them. They worked swiftly and moved everything worth moving into Buddy and Erika's garage in Killeen, twenty minutes away.

I heard from different members of the moving party how they were all struck by the appearance of certain things in the apartment. They told me how there was an open book by the rocking chair, two plates at the table, and bacon in a frying pan still on the stove. The burner had been turned off, but nothing had been put away. They said it looked as if God had walked in while my parents were preparing breakfast and simply said, "It's time to go." And they obeyed.

Seeking Closure

I believe it was moving day or the day after that a handful of the police officers and state troopers took Allan, Erika, and me to dinner at a local café, and we got the full story of Mom's final moments. I believe they desperately needed to share with us what really went on in those last few minutes of the incident, for the newspapers were filled with rumors and misrepresentations of the facts.

They told us many of the officers had actually been attending a seminar at the Sheraton when they were radioed about the shootings just one building over. In what turned out to be a unique example of the idiocy of gun control, the hotel management had asked the policemen to leave their weapons locked in their cars. They were concerned other guests might feel uncomfortable with all of those guns in plain view. So after they received the call, several minutes were wasted retrieving weapons from the trunks of their cars and getting them loaded.

Once at Luby's, they quickly set up a perimeter, but were at a huge disadvantage due to the same backlighting issue I had encountered when I tried to look inside for my mom. For the most part, they could only see silhouettes and shadows. Bravely risking his own life, one of the officers entered the building at the broken front window near the rear end of the truck which he used as his shield. He was quickly followed by two of his comrades.

At first, they did not know who the bad guy was and could only wait and watch. Precious seconds ticked by. The scene had changed drastically from how it started. It had turned chaotic, as people were attempting to escape, and it made locating the perpetrator momentarily impossible. Apparently, my mother had deliberately stayed behind and had crawled out into the open to be with my father.

The officers' eyes were drawn to where she knelt, cradling my father's head in her lap. It was then they discovered who the bad guy was. They saw him walk to where

Mom sat stroking her husband's brow. He glared down at her. She glanced up at him as he put the muzzle of his gun to her head. She looked down at her husband once more, and he pulled the trigger.

It had not occurred to me at the time, but they had just had their 47th anniversary. Mom was not going anywhere without Dad.

The officers went on to explain how all they had to do was fire a shot into the ceiling, and the "a--hole rabbitted" to a bathroom alcove area. Instead of being able to continue his deadly rampage, he revealed his own cowardice in his final acts. The few cops who had made their way into the dining area crawled over chairs, tables, and bodies in an effort to get a better shot at the murderer.

One trooper told us with tears in his eyes that Dad grabbed his hand as he crawled by and made an effort to sit up. He said he quickly explained to him they were still exchanging fire, and it wasn't safe yet. He told us Dad was cognizant enough to understand. So he lay back down, but squeezed the officer's hand hard with his own bloodied one and said, "It hurts." The officer removed his hand from Dad's grip and told him, "I understand. Let us finish this, and we'll get right back to you."

They had continued to move in on the murderer. A few admitted to us they had made solemn vows he would not come out of that restaurant to see a trial. They managed to hit him once or twice, but the wounds were not life-threatening. It all ended when, in a final act of defiance or cowardice—I don't know which—the madman rolled onto his back and put a bullet into his own brain.

Either way, he was not going to come out alive. In the end, he saved us all the trouble and expense of a trial or prison.

Newspapers, television reporters, and even some survivors and their families questioned and generally Monday-morning-quarterbacked the officers' response to the shootings. But I am convinced, amidst all of the chaos, those first responders did the very best job they could with the information they had.

Many of the people involved have gone on to train other first-responder teams across the country. But some of them were so affected by the tragedy they soon left their chosen profession for good. One officer told me he had seen heavy fighting in Vietnam, but he did not expect the war zone he found when he entered his local eatery. It was too much for him to bear.

On Monday, Greg and I began the three-hour drive to San Antonio for the burial. On the way, we stopped at a little diner in Johnson City, one-time home to President Lyndon Baines Johnson. The café was a cute little place on the main highway that runs through an otherwise sleepy town. We sat in a booth and ordered dinner. While we waited and made small talk, a waitress across the tiny room dropped a tray full of glasses and plates. The loud crash made everyone jump. But my heart leapt to my throat, and my adrenalin surged. I reached for my purse and its newly replaced gun in an instant. Thankfully, I quickly realized my error and never retrieved the gun.

As my heart rate began to return to normal, Greg and I looked around the room and realized it could not happen there anyway. There were maybe a dozen customers, and I would have been willing to bet at least three or four of them were armed. No, they were not Hell's Angels. They were just regular Texans who looked like they were used to taking care of themselves.

Greg and I realized two very important things that evening. The first was that if a nut had gone in and started shooting, he would get only two or three rounds off before someone took him down. Second, no one looking for a high body-bag count would have tried it in there to begin with. Any idiot could have been pretty certain that more than one potential victim was armed and, not having any way of knowing which guys were carrying, had to have a huge deterrent effect.

A fter heavy family debate and split votes, Allan, Erika, and I actually decided to do a taped satellite interview for the Maury Povich show on the morning of the interment. Dressed for the funeral—I had chosen another dress my Mom had made—we sat in a San Antonio studio with little audio wires plugged into our ears and stared into a blank television camera.

I quickly learned to avoid satellite feeds if at all possible. It is difficult to hear all of the conversation going on in the main studio, and you do not have the visual feedback so necessary to a normal conversation. If adversarial, it can make your side of an argument appear less clever or intelligent.

Unlike the guests they had in their New York studio, we were not provided with television makeup. Trust me: it makes a difference. Viewers tend to have less confidence in someone who appears a little shiny, oily, or lacking in color.

But, we were "victims" on our way to our parents' burial. So, I am reasonably sure the viewers cut us some slack. We were slowly realizing a faction of society was already beginning to use those cafeteria murders as an example of the need for more gun control. It had been hinted at in some of the telephone interviews I had done, and it was beginning to creep into this television talk show with questions from their New York audience.

I was already getting a bit agitated when someone asked what struck me as an incredibly stupid question—something along the lines of, "Well, Miss Gratia, I don't believe you would have been capable of using your gun in

that situation. You don't really know how you would have reacted, and other people could have gotten hurt. I think more guns would have just made things worse."

I think my pupils must have dilated and my ears flamed red as I barely contained myself and tersely blurted back something like, "Ma'am, at that time I was in complete control of my emotions, and I have hit much smaller targets at much greater distances. The only thing the gun control laws did was prevent me from protecting my family. But, there is one thing even you cannot deny: having a gun sure would have changed the odds, wouldn't it?!" I was furious at this twit for suggesting something so stupid.

Later, when it aired, I was floored to discover my "Ma'am" was a "Sir." How embarrassing. But friends and family quickly pointed out there was no way for me to know, without benefit of a television monitor, the effeminate looking and sounding person was, indeed, a man.

After leaving the studio, we continued on to Fort Sam Houston and the burial site. Allan and Kathy's pastor had done his homework and performed a beautiful graveside service and eulogized my parents to the best of his ability. My boyfriend, Greg, sat with me in full dress Army uniform and had arranged for a twenty-one-gun salute. He stood at attention and saluted as they continued on into a rendition of "Taps." I distinctly recall feeling a soft breeze across my cheek near the end of that incredibly sad refrain. I was certain that it was my parents' last caress on their way to another place. Erika later told me she had felt it as well.

Mom and Dad were buried that beautiful day in a gravesite overlooking a golf course.

CHAPTER 9
Controlling the Message

Upon returning to the Lampasas/Copperas Cove area the next day, I recall wishing I could rush back to my office and start right back into seeing patients. But of course, even though it was something I wanted to do, I knew my patients and staff would not let me. I knew that every time one of them walked through the door they would naturally want to give their condolences, along with a hug or some other show of affection. I just did not want to deal with any more of that for a while.

My choices seemed either to sit around the house and mope, or seek some distraction elsewhere. It occurred to me that the trip I had planned with Mom to Albuquerque was still intact. The interment was on a Monday, and our flight was to be on Wednesday. Erika was not ready to go back to her classroom and teach, and she was an Arabian horse enthusiast, as well. So it took very little prodding for her to agree to join me on what was supposed to be Mom's birthday trip.

She actually had to carry a copy of one of the newspaper articles, naming our mother as one of the dead, to be able to use her plane tickets. We still did not have a death certificate of any sort from the coroner's office, so it was a bit tricky. But, I think the sheer magnitude of the event was still heavy in the public's minds, so no airline personnel wanted to ask too many questions or make a fuss, although you could tell that bending their rules was out of their collective comfort zone.

The short plane ride to Albuquerque was just what the doctor ordered for both of us. We knew a few people at the Arabian Horse National Championships well enough that polite and heartfelt words were occasionally exchanged, but it certainly was not the constant barrage we would have received had we been at our respective workplaces. The newspapers, however, continued their coverage for many days.

There were stories written from every conceivable angle. Some profiled the killer; many profiled the victims. Family members continued to forward interview requests to our hotel message center. We each granted a few over the phone while still in New Mexico. Someone told us Paul Harvey, the well-known radio celebrity, actually based one of his shows, entitled "The Rest of the Story," on our parents and the love and devotion they clearly shared to the end. I was moved by the knowledge that my parents' lives and deaths had meaning to so many strangers, and I wish I could have heard the segment.

When we returned home several days later, I immediately headed back to work. I relished the continued distraction. My brain constantly rehashed the event, and I hoped enough time had passed to lighten the load of condolences that would still be given. I did not want to find myself bursting into tears every time a patient hugged me.

Sharing the Grief

I believe it was the City of Killeen, or perhaps the Bell County Crime Victims unit, that hosted a sort of post-trauma briefing in the weeks that followed. Quite a few people attended.

Although I really did not want to go, in the end I was very glad I did. Being raised to be self-reliant, I never understood the attraction of group therapy. But I can tell you now, I was amazed at how comforting it was to hear other people sharing stories and thought patterns similar to my own. Even simple things, like knowing that many others who had been there that day would be startled beyond the norm at loud noises: especially the sound of breaking glass. There was that feeling of relief in knowing you were not the only one experiencing crazy stuff.

It helped hearing other people's perspectives on what happened that day, to be able to get the story straight in my own head and to fill in the inevitable gaps. It was interesting to find out how differently some people reacted to the same situation. I knew most of the patrons located near my parents and me in that front corner of the restaurant died that day. But some did not.

I asked one how she survived, but she did not know. She said she lay on the floor with her back to the killer and hid her face against the baseboard. Apparently he simply passed over her. There was another young woman who told me she hid under a bench in the serving line next to a stranger. She said that as the gunman moved down the line toward them, the stranger looked at her and very calmly and pointedly said, "*You* are going to be all right." The gunman shot the stranger just inches from her and then passed her by.

I later learned the stranger was named Connie, and she was another chiropractor, from the Austin area, who had been out for a joy ride on her motorcycle. Her surviving buffet-line neighbor said Connie had just seemed to know. Although she had graduated from Texas Chiropractic College before my brother and I, it was a fairly small school, so I am pretty sure we had met Connie in those years past.

One very interesting aspect of it all was the different effect it had on friends and family who were not in the restaurant, but whose lives were, nonetheless, changed forever. My boyfriend, Greg, was overwhelmed at being on the edge of a tragedy, yet being at a loss for knowing what to do. He found out he was not alone.

In fact, I think in many ways it was actually harder on close friends or family who were not at the cafeteria that day. No matter how many times they heard the story, it could not be fully grasped without having been there: the sights, the sounds, the layout, the timing, all of the things the brain could take in when it was real, but could not be fully shared. I know that Greg, Buddy, and Allan simply could not grasp how such a situation could take place without the bad guy being rushed and tackled by the good guys.

Try as I would to explain it, I could not seem to get across to them the control that the killer was able to exert due to the spacing of tables and diners. Although every seat had been filled, it was not wall-to-wall people, bumping into each other and obscuring the murderer's view. Nor could you coordinate an attack; there simply was not the time. For several minutes, the gunman had complete control.

I think that is particularly difficult for men to grasp. I would draw pictures of the cafeteria layout and show where we had been seated, where the truck had entered, and other details I thought were important. I would try to explain what happened where, but it just did not fill in all of the blanks for them. They fully realized that they were armchair quarterbacking.

One of the things I believe was the most helpful to Buddy, Erika, and Greg happened when the crime victims unit notified us that the restaurant would be opening the doors to us for an evening. I think it was suggested to the corporate office that it would help many people with what the psychologists like to call closure.

They were careful to assure us no media would be allowed and the evidence of the slaughter had been removed. That is a polite way of saying that the carpet had been taken up and the concrete flooring had been pressure washed. I was somewhat reluctant to return to the scene. The pain was too fresh. But I realized what benefit it could have for the others of my family, so I agreed to give them a narration.

After arriving at the eerily empty restaurant, I walked the three of them through the events of that day. I showed them where we sat, where the gunman walked, where

Dad made his attack, and where he fell with the gunshot wound. I was able to show them where I had tried to get Mom on her feet and even the boarded up window through which I was able to escape.

The cleaning crew had not done such a complete job on the asphalt just outside the front door, where Dad had laid on the stretcher and bled out. My sister spotted the stain, but maintained composure. They each said the walk-through had been the most important factor in answering the many questions lingering in their minds. I wish my brother could have gone with us that night. I think it would have helped him a lot in those initial weeks and months.

Telling the Story

The one aspect of post-killings life that did surprise me was the ongoing media interest. I expected it to slow down much more rapidly than it did. Of course, over time, it did change. Each reporter or radio host who called had a different direction they wanted to take their story. I am not sure why I got so many more calls than the other witnesses to the crime, but I suspect it was due in large part to two things: I had spouted off about the gun laws in a way they did not expect, and I was willing to talk to them about it.

Sometimes I think those reporters who have to get interviews after such awful crimes are so grateful to any-one who will talk to them they will bend over backwards to be polite and kind. Despite what you may have heard, I also believe the majority of them are indeed human and have compassion. Interviewing victims is not a fun part of their job.

My criteria for granting interviews changed with that realization. They also changed, in large part, due to the influence of a brilliant, insightful, and very influential man named Neal Knox, who tracked me down shortly after the airing of the Povich show. At the time, he was one of the big wigs with the National Rifle Association, but he also had a more personal connection to the ordeal that convinced me to have lunch with him: he was from Lampasas.

His parents had a ranch not far from my little place and, as if that were not enough, two of his brother's coworkers were killed in the restaurant that day. In fact, his brother Rusty should have been there too, but had opted to wait behind at the office for a client who was running late. Once his client arrived, they hopped into a car and drove over to Luby's, but decided it was too crowded and their co-workers would probably be nearly done. So, they drove two blocks further down the road to Red Lobster.

Neal knew he could have lost his brother, and that gave him credibility in my mind.

He contacted me at my clinic and asked me to lunch. We had a long conversation during which I realized he was not a mere talking head for a large organization, but that he deeply and religiously held the same principles as my father regarding, not only the Bill of Rights, but many other concepts as well. I immediately liked and trusted him.

Asserting Second Amendment Rights

He had seen that Maury Povich show and had apparently liked what he heard me say. Neal wanted to know if I was willing to do more interviews and speeches on the subject of our Second Amendment rights. I was still very angry, both at myself, for having made what was a stupid decision to follow an even stupider law, and at my legislators for creating that law. Speaking to whoever would listen was a great way of venting that anger. So, I told him I would make myself available as the need arose. But, I told Neal, I drew the line at the really sleazy talk shows like "Geraldo," whose producers, coincidently, had called me earlier that day and invited me to do their show.

Neal quickly clarified things for me in a way I recalled many times thereafter. He said, "How many times can you go on national TV and have an audience of millions? It doesn't matter what kind of garbage the host spews or what he may ask you. You can say whatever you want, so that you can get your message across to the kind of people who would never hear that side of the story otherwise."

Good point. But it was "Geraldo!" Ick! At that time, he was the king of sleaze! Remarkably, that type of show actually got much worse before the public sickened of them.

Neal continued his convincing.

"When are you ever going to get that stay-at-home mom, welfare recipient, or spoon-fed liberal to hear something other than the usual media diatribe about the evils of guns? And, not just from some egghead spouting statistics, but from someone who was an actual victim."

God, I hated that word.

Once again, his point was well made. People who have an opinion about something considered controversial usually end up preaching to the choir. I had already figured out that debating the anti-self-defense crowd was much more fun. I especially loved going up against whiners who had never had to defend themselves or who depended upon someone else to do it. "Why don't you just call 9-1-1? That's what the police are for."

So I was convinced. From that day on, I said yes to nearly any talk show, sleazy or otherwise, that would pay my expenses, which included a doctor to cover my practice for the one- or two-day trips. I heard once, through the local grapevine, that people thought I was getting paid ten thousand bucks a show, and that was the primary reason I did them. To put it bluntly: Dang, I wish!

In reality, I never made a penny. Those shows may pay some people, but not a nobody "victim" from Texas. After a while, I did start insisting that they fly me on an airline that kept my frequent flier miles. I figured I could at least eventually get a free trip to someplace fun out of the deal.

Of course there were non-sleazy, legitimate news or entertainment shows as well. One of the first ones I was involved with, in a very small way, was "America's Most Wanted" with John Walsh. He invited several of us who were in the restaurant that day to do a show. He brought his crew to Killeen, and they were all incredibly gracious.

I think talking about such a dreadful incident in a group situation was very cathartic for several participants. It may have even been therapeutic for Mr. Walsh, as he became teary-eyed when he shared with us the story of Adam. You see Adam was his very young son who was kidnapped from a Sears store at the age of six. Some fishermen found the boy's severed head a week or so later, and his little body was found some time after that.

I cannot imagine, nor do I even want to try to comprehend, that father's depth of pain. When he finished his story, he explained how it was that tragedy that spurred him on to create "America's Most Wanted." That very popular show has aided in the capture of many murderers, kidnappers, robbers, and other assorted predators. More importantly, their removal from society has undoubtedly prevented an untold number of tragedies for other families.

What an incredible legacy Adam has left us, but at such a terrible price.

When taping the show on the Luby's cafeteria shooting was complete, Mr. Walsh hosted a barbecue for the participants and their families. It was a comfortable thing where host and guests alike shared an unspoken bond. It created a pleasant memory in the midst of tragedy.

During the days surrounding the taping of the show, my brother made an interesting observation. Sometimes when horrible tragedies befall people, they find themselves wondering why every newspaper and television show has to capture each little detail and continuously rehash the painful or tragic story. We have seen it after hurricanes, floods, tornadoes, and human-caused disasters.

Allan believed that it was our very human quality of feeling compassion, as well as our need to feel a connectedness to something bigger than ourselves. And when it is a tragedy that befalls a large number of people, you can almost bet nearly everyone in the country is within only one or two degrees of separation from the victims or near-victims. They either know somebody, or know somebody who knows somebody, who was there that day. And they probably all experience a momentary sense of "There, but for the grace of God, go I."

Unintended Consequences

Another one of the first few shows we agreed to be part of was "48 Hours." They did a pretty good job of imparting some meaning to such a seemingly senseless act. And once again it made me feel good that my parents' lives had meaning to other people. Unfortunately, there was one very unintended consequence of doing that show. In the days following the murders, my sister-in-law, Kathy, had done her best to notify as many friends and family as possible. Of course, she was unable to reach everyone, and none of us thought to continue with follow-up calls or letters.

Immediately following the "48 Hours" airing, I received a call from a lady in Florida with whom my mother had grown up in Wisconsin. They had remained close, although geographically distant. Although I had met her only a few times, she and my mom were like sisters. In fact Terri had come to visit Mom just months prior to the shootings. She and her husband had been watching the show when it displayed pictures and names of all of the cafeteria victims. Of course, both Mom and Dad were up on the screen. Poor Terri could not believe her ears and eyes!

I felt terrible that that was the way she learned about her dear friend's passing. I begged her forgiveness for not following up on our contacts. Of course, she understood, but I can only imagine how difficult that must have been for her.

Terri kept tabs on me and the rest of her friend's brood until her death some years later. Shortly before her own passing, she gifted me with an extraordinary teapot Mom had given her as a wedding present many years earlier. It was not anything fancy, but the warm feelings and fond memories that came with it were invaluable.

Requests for interviews continued to pour in. I did appear on the "Geraldo" show some little time after Terri's call. True to his 1990s form, Geraldo did his best to elicit some tears and drama from me. He even went so far as to actually ask me if I had cried since my parents' death. I told him, "Yes," but I felt it was something to do in private, and it was not what I was on his show to do. Neal Knox's words were still ringing in my ears and reminding me that I could control my own message.

I knew I had an audience largely made up of liberal-types, who had always been told that guns were inherently evil and we needed more and more restrictive laws on gun ownership and usage. No one had to tell me that the vast majority of the audience at that studio, or those who would eventually watch from home, had been to public schools that had not taught them history or any of the real reasons for our Second Amendment. I certainly could not give them a remedial course in my five minutes on the show, but I hoped I could tell them my story in a way that would draw them in and cause them to be empathetic toward me.

After telling of my parents' violent end, I tried to explain to them that, in fact, there was nothing to stop a madman from coming into the studio at that moment and committing the same horrible crime. If not in the studio, then perhaps later on in the day, after they picked up their kids from daycare and stopped at their favorite café to grab a snack. Could they imagine what that would be like? I wanted them to understand, at the gut level, how awful it would be to be caught in that kind of situation and have no way to protect themselves or their kids. I wanted to show them they have the right and, indeed, the responsibility to protect themselves and their families.

To my amazement, it seemed many audience members responded favorably to my little twist on the typical gun-banning tripe they had been fed all their lives. I sensed that it made them hesitate in their usual line of thinking. After all, I had standing in their view. I was not a talking head spouting history or statistics. I was a victim.

I did my best that day to use that authority to change some minds.

CHAPTER 10
Testifying for
the Right to Carry

Life goes on, and the world keeps turning.

Several years have passed since October 16th, 1991. I married that man who saluted my parents and held my hand through many grief-stricken days. We have had three boys, one of whom died after only five days on this earth. But we were somewhat fortunate: an ultrasound performed halfway through the pregnancy warned us of the impending doom and allowed us to prepare our first two children and ourselves for little Aaron's quiet death.

We had already learned that sometimes fate is not so kind. Sometimes you don't get to say "goodbye."

It wasn't long after our third son's passing that a woman approached me at my local bank. She said, "You don't know me, but my daughter was one of the young women killed in Luby's that day." She told me her daughter's name, and I recognized it as one on the list of the dead. That poor woman's daughter had been shot in the head, at point-blank range.

The lady in the bank continued, "I wanted to let you know I really appreciate the stance you have been taking about guns in your interviews. You probably didn't know it, but Sara (not her real name) had a gun in her car, too. Oh, how I wish she had been able to carry it that day!"

I couldn't think of anything to say. So I just thanked her for her kind words and for letting me know of that small but important detail in her life.

During the years following the death of my parents, I received a lot of grateful responses to many of my interviews. It seemed I was giving a voice to what many people had been thinking about gun legislation, but had no public venue for expression. I had many different kinds of folks from all areas of the country and even abroad contacting me. Most thanked me for lending a public voice to their views. A few, rarely, chastised me for my gun-related opinions. But those letters or phone calls were few and far between and were greatly outnumbered by the "atta-girls."

I always suspected that the reluctance of people to send nasty letters to me was most likely due to my victim status. I suppose it would be hard to speak out against someone who has lived through such a nightmarish situation. I suppose it would be vaguely like a politician asserting a soldier did not respond properly in the heat of battle. I think they recognize they would sound silly if they had not been on the battlefield themselves. Nobody likes or respects an armchair quarterback.

Many people contacted me in the hope that I held the same strong opinions regarding our other inherent and constitutional rights. Of course, with my background and upbringing, I did, but did not usually have an opportunity to speak about them. Through it all, there were many times I was asked to run for state or national office. I think when folks believe they have found someone who thinks like they do, they would like that person to represent them in government.

The issue of elected office was a little bit of a sore spot for me. You see, my Dad always hoped one of us would run for office and help wrestle the subject of his own book into law. I hoped it would be my brother. Allan had a political bent for as long as I could remember, and he had always been a great speaker and debater. I know he had considered it long before Dad was killed, but for various reasons had chosen not to run for any office.

Although I had been thrust into the media soup pot and had never backed away from a good debate, I really had other things to do in my life. I liked making money. Members of the Texas Legislature made a whopping six hundred dollars a month—more like one hundred and twenty, after taxes and insurance—and, although it was supposed to be a part-time job, it seemed to suck up all their time.

The competitive nature in me always wanted to run for Congress and win. Although the federal legislature made far more money, I did not want to raise kids in Washington, D.C. I liked living in my little house in Texas, with my family, friends, horses, and view. No. Washington was definitely not for me.

Concealed-Carry Licensing

During those years, the issue of concealed-carry licensing was a hot topic in Texas. Jerry Patterson was a state senator then, and he carried legislation that would have mimicked the new Florida concealed-carry law. It consisted of a required short course on the applicable statutes, fingerprinting and background check, a proficiency test, some fees, and meeting the basic federal requirements for gun ownership. Florida had had a huge increase in violent crime over the prior few years. To their credit, they were seeking ways to let good people protect themselves, since there was no possible way to hire enough law-enforcement officers to cover everyone all the time.

In an interesting twist, after their law was enacted, Florida bad guys started hijacking rental cars on their way from the airports. Most of those guys wanted easy targets, and they knew visitors getting off planes would not be armed.

I have always tried to make it clear that I do not like the idea of concealed-carry licensing: requiring people to jump through hoops and receive a permit to be able to exercise a right strikes me as counterproductive. The very idea that I have to ask "permission," of which "permit" is just a variant, from the government to be able to protect myself is foreign to me. I mean really foreign, like something you would have to do in Pol Pot's regime, not in the freedom-loving USA.

But I am a pragmatist. I recognize we have not lost those American rights all at once. They have been slowly nibbled away while we were not looking. I believe restoration of those rights will probably happen incrementally as well. So anything that moves the bar in our favor is something I am likely to support. That is why I generally support concealed-carry permit legislation. It moves the bar in the right direction.

There are groups, for which I have great respect, that encourage a different approach. Theirs is an all-or-nothing strategy. Although I agree wholeheartedly with their basic philosophy, I simply don't believe it is workable most of the time. I am thrilled they are out there, however, because they are loudly speaking the truth! Other associations are politically astute, but often seem to drown their own message in minutiae, and the over-arching concept of *right* is lost in political pragmatism.

So it has always been with some reservation that I testify in favor of concealed-carry bills before a legislature. I spoke to a Texas House committee during a public hearing for Senator Patterson's bill and did my best to swing a vote or two. I do not know with certainty that it was my testimony that made the difference, but I like to think I played a small role in getting that bill passed.

It went to Democrat Governor Ann Richards, who vetoed it. To this day, I believe her decision to veto played a major role in eventually putting George W. Bush in the White House. You see concealed-carry permitting was a huge issue in the following gubernatorial race that pitted the two against each other. Bush made it clear: if the Texas Legislature could get a similar bill to his desk, he would sign it. That declaration rallied the troops, and the pro-gun, pro-self-defense people came out of the woodwork at voting time. Of course, Bush won.

Testifying for Change

Thereafter, another bill, authored by Jerry Patterson on the Senate side and Bill Carter and Ron Wilson on the House side, made its way through the process in the '95 session. Representative Wilson made an amazing proponent for concealed carry as a black, inner-city Democrat, who was a widely acknowledged expert on the House rules, and without a doubt, one of the finest debaters I have ever been privileged to hear. A knife-wielding assailant had once attacked his wife. I think he never wanted her to be without protection again.

Representative Carter, on the other hand, was a quiet, unassuming fatherly figure people liked and respected. He did not easily fly off the handle. But it was Patterson who deftly steered the bill around all the potholes and roadblocks. Although I never heard of him raising his voice, I have seen him cut his opponents to the bone with a wit so sharp they were unaware they were even bleeding, until it was too late. Some of his victims would even crack a smile as they withered.

It was Patterson who asked me to testify for his bill before a Senate committee. The hearing took place in the Senate chambers, not a hearing room, with several of the legislators seated around a long, rectangular table. The chairman sat at the head of the table, and witnesses sat opposite him. Since this was a high-profile bill, the area surrounding the table was crowded with television cameras and reporters, hoping to get something juicy for their stations or papers. I had already begun to figure out the way to get any of these legislators to change their vote on an issue was to get the press and, as a result, their constituents to be passionate in their support of a change.

I asked Senator Patterson's aide to point out the gentleman who was most vocal in his opposition to the bill. It happened to be a black Democrat from the inner-city Dallas area, who was built like an NFL linebacker and was known to use his size to intimidate his foes. I was reasonably sure I would not change his views on the matter, but I wanted to use him as camera fodder. What I mean is that you could bet that the six and ten o'clock news would air the most controversial ten seconds of footage they got from the hearing. I wanted to do my best to illustrate the crux of the argument in those few moments.

After roll was called and Senator Patterson explained his bill, the chairman began the task of calling for public testimony. Since I had been invited, I was one of the first to speak for the bill. After taking my seat across from the chairman, I thanked the members for the opportunity to testify, and then began telling them my story in a way I had hoped would play on their emotions.

I asked the chairman if I could stand up and use some dramatics to demonstrate what happened to my family on that day in October. He politely agreed to my request. After giving a detailed account of the event, I asked them to put themselves in my place. I told them to imagine, for a moment, what it would be like for them to take a break from the hearing and have lunch together at some favorite restaurant near the Capitol. In fact, I pointed out to them, the weather outside was beautiful and very similar to that autumn day to which I referred. It was also a similar time of day. As they are finishing their lunch, someone enters the dining area and slowly, methodically pulls out a gun and begins executing people.

As my new story unfolded, I was "slowly and methodically" walking around the table with my hand held up as if it were a gun: thumb and forefinger extended, the last three fingers curled into my palm. I explained how easy it was to exert control when you are the only one with the gun. I mimicked how the gunman would execute those present by simply pointing and pulling the trigger, stepping to the next, pointing and pulling the trigger, all the while narrating the act.

As I crept down the long side of the table, across from the senators, I was fully conscious of the cameras rolling their tape just over my shoulder. I mock-shot two or three senators, then brought my recoiling gun down to within a few feet of the Dallas senator's face, pretending to take dead aim at his forehead. He saw it coming, however, and immediately yelled at me to "get that finger out of my face!!!"

I withdrew my hand, apologized to the chairman, and continued by asking, "At that point, Senator, don't you wish you, or someone around you, had a gun and knew how to use it?" He was very angry, but the point was made, and the cameras caught it. What I really wanted to ask him was "if my pointed finger makes you nervous, you pompous jackass, imagine what it is like to stare down the barrel of a 9 mm like my parents did in their very last moments on Earth!" Fortunately, I thought better of it, thanked the members for their indulgence, and sat down. I wanted him to come across as the aggressor against me. After all, I was the "victim" and had asked for, and received, permission for the dramatic interpretation.

Although a vote was not immediately taken, the legislation did eventually pass, and Governor George W. Bush signed it into law. It took effect in January 1996 and put the bad guys on notice with a clear message: from now on in Texas, we want the good guys to win!

❖ ❖ ❖

CHAPTER 11
The Candidate

It took a few years before Greg and I got into the financial position where we could entertain the idea of my going to Austin and joining the ranks of state lawmakers. In January 1996 I filed for State Representative for District 54. Throughout the next several months I campaigned using the Ronald Reagan model: choose only three or four primary campaign issues and repeatedly hammer on them.

None of the issues I chose had to do with guns. I correctly guessed that anyone who was going to base their vote on that issue alone already knew who I was and what I had done for the Texas effort. While my opponent's camp tried to peg me as a one-issue candidate, I never brought it up. When guns rights were referred to or asked about in debates, I responded to questions or comments. But I always let them bring up the subject. The notion that I was a one-issue candidate fizzled quickly.

My opponent was a good man and similarly pro-gun anyway, so we just could not help the audience delineate between the two of us using a firearms debate. Instead, we concentrated on other topics where our differences became clearer. He was a gentleman, and I believe he actually enjoyed the campaigning as much as I did. We were able to stand in front of the crowds and say, "We like each other. We have some differences of opinion on how the state should be run. Here are those differences. Now it is up to you to choose."

Wouldn't it be nice if all campaigns were run that way?

On the first Tuesday in November, the stars aligned for me, and I became the next State Representative Elect from District 54. It has been an interesting ride ever since that night. I was sworn into the legislature, and in January I hit the ground running. I quickly found that, even in my newly elected position, I initially had to distance myself somewhat from gun bills. While I needed to establish myself as someone who would fight equally for all of our rights, there were still many times I felt compelled to weigh in on firearms legislation. House members and constituents expected it.

Over a period of time, nearly every new member of the legislature carves out certain niches, or areas of expertise, for themselves. Sometimes it is a by-product of their background, and other times it comes from hours spent on the committees to which they are assigned. No one can be an expert on everything that comes to the floor for a vote. So members quickly learn to rely on friends who have similar political philosophies, but different areas of knowledge.

Whether I liked it or not, most gun legislation was brought to me for review and blessing. That is not to say I was the be-all-end-all on the issue—not by any stretch of the imagination. I think my status came as a result of media attention. I was recognized as a driving force on that topic and could help an author predict problems or traps that might occur.

On the flip side, I could help kill a bill outright. And since much of what legislators accomplish while in office is based on relationships they have formed, I would also let an author know if I would speak against his bill, in case I saw no way of making it more acceptable. Sometimes the very concept behind a draft of legislation was flawed beyond repair. So it was only fair to give the author a heads-up that I would be voting against or even openly fighting his proposed law.

Of course that was not always enough to make the bill go away. The other legislator may, in fact, have had more votes on his side. But I found that being up front about my stance on a subject was generally appreciated and respected. Nobody likes a sneak.

Ethan, (then Governor) George W. Bush, Alex, me, and Greg.

Most of the time, we go through life not knowing if we have had any effect on other peoples' opinions or decisions. In contrast, after a vigorous debate in the House of Representatives or Senate, one's views on a subject are typically posted for all to see, via the voting process. If you are involved in the debate, you quickly discover the outcome of your persuasiveness. It should make most of my readers happy that so many of their own opinions are not put on display for public scrutiny and judgment!

One evening when we had adjourned for the day, I attended a dinner that the committee chairman was giving for his members. It was a tradition that often proved helpful in forging bonds and smoothing ruffled feathers. One of my fellow committee members, Keith Oakley, was also the Chairman of the House Committee on Public Safety, before which I stood in 1993 as a citizen testifying for the gun bill that ultimately had been vetoed. He shared a story I will never forget.

Where Politics Meets the Pavement

He reminded me it had been up to him whether to even grant a hearing for that initial concealed-carry bill. Frankly, he said, he had been on the fence about the issue from day one. Of course, he eventually held a public hearing at which I was invited to speak. He said my testimony made the difference for him. Not only would he let the bill come to a committee vote, but he would even be an "aye."

As a rural, white Democrat, whose constituents were farmers and ranchers, he believed it was the right thing to do. But most of the inner-city and minority Democrats, as well as the law-enforcement agency heads, which he oversaw as Chairman of the Public Safety Committee, were almost entirely against the bill.

Democrat Governor Ann Richards prided herself on being publicly pro-gun and pro-hunter. But she knew this bill could put her in a very vulnerable position with the Democrat base. So she summoned Keith to her office. After some initial small talk, she very pointedly said, "You can't let this bill out of your committee. You need to kill it now."

He said, "Governor, I can't do that. My whole district supports this. If I want to get reelected, I've got to let it out of committee. Why don't we make it a referendum, and let the people vote on it?"

The Governor replied, "Just because the people vote for it, doesn't make it right."

To which Keith said, in his oh-so-subtle way, "I'm sorry…. I've obviously got this democracy sh-t all mixed up."

With that, she abruptly stood up behind her desk and said, "I thought you were my friend."

"I came here as your friend."

"You have given me no workable scenario!"

Oakley stood up and said, "Well, I'm sorry. Goodbye," and turned and left the office.

He was so shocked at her attempt to kill the process that he left the Capitol somewhat shaken and unsure of his next move. He sat in his car out in a parking area, staring up at Lady Liberty atop the pink granite dome. It was very late at night, and the lights played on the United States and Texas flags as they waved in the springtime breeze. As he sat pondering his next move, it occurred to him that she was not at all concerned about *his* reelection. She was trying to cover her own backside in a behind-the-scenes way that would have left him as the scapegoat. The realization made him angry and even more determined to do the right thing.

Just a couple of nights later, another committee that Keith was a member of finished its work late. He found himself leaving the Capitol around 2 a.m. and heading for his apartment. He described his place to me as "not in the best part of town."

As he pulled into the parking area, he noticed a tall, burly young man with a bandana around his neck looking suspiciously into a parked car. When he spotted Keith, he immediately moved away from that car in a guilty fashion, and it seemed as if he was just going to keep walking down the sidewalk. As Keith stepped out of his vehicle, the big guy stepped toward him instead, got right in his face and said, "Hey man, you got the time?"

Rattled by the man's sudden proximity and certainty that he was not really interested in the time, it made Keith react with some abruptness, telling him, "I got all the time I need."

The man looked irritated, moved still closer and said, "No, man, the time. You got the time?"

Keith did his best to look bigger and said, "Yeah. I got all night."

The man turned away cursing, then seemed to have second thoughts and turned back appearing angry and animated. Waving his arms wildly, he yelled, "What the f--k are you lookin' at?"

Keith immediately reached his hand around to the small of his back and acted as if he were going to pull out a gun, at the same time saying, "Man, you better get out of here while you've got the chance!"

The hoodlum stopped so suddenly he may as well have hit a brick wall. He said, "What are you, the f--ing police?"

To which Keith replied, "Yes I am, and let me tell you, you're about this close to spending the night in jail!"

Now, of course we all know that it is completely illegal to impersonate a police officer. So I feel it is incumbent upon me to point out that Keith thought the thug meant "Police" with a capital "P," and that he was being asked if he were part of the popular rock band.

The man quickly began backing up and waving his arms in front of his face, "You got nothin' on me! You got nothin' on me!" Then he turned away and moved quickly down the street.

It was an epiphany for Keith Oakley: He knew exactly what he was going to do with that gun bill the Governor did not want to come to a House vote. The decision was made in an instant and with absolute clarity of thought. This was not about party politics. This was about self-defense. The next day he went out and bought the biggest, loudest handgun he could comfortably carry and has kept it with him ever since.

I was amazed by the story he revealed to me and humbled to have had a small hand in his initial decision to let his committee vote on the bill. On the larger matter of letting the bill leave his hands and continue its journey against the Governor's wishes, his gutsy decision and the chain of events he unknowingly set into motion left me awestruck.

Texas Speaker of the House Tom Craddick presented a gavel to Ethan on his birthday, and the entire House of Representatives sang Happy Birthday to him as Alex and I looked on.

The bill did indeed pass both the House and Senate, only to be vetoed by the Governor. I believe it was the single issue in the next campaign that sent her opponents to the polling booths to vote against her and for George W. Bush. Had he not become Texas's next governor, would he have made it to the White House? How would our history have been altered? Was that scary guy in the parking lot just a working man looking for the time, or were his intentions more sinister?

Or if you believe in angels, was he just the catalyst that was needed to get the historical ball rolling? Perhaps I am blowing the entire flow of events out of proportion, but if you believe things happen for a reason, then you must wonder about the ripple effects of each little pebble.

I like Keith's explanation. When I asked him if he thought his actions may have set the stage for something much bigger, he replied with a glint in his eye and in his usual sardonic tone, "Yes, I'm the guy responsible for the war in Iraq."

❖ ❖ ❖

CHAPTER 12
The So-Called
Million Mom March

In 1999 five very feisty women were locked in an Internet gripe session regarding a newly formed, and very vocal, anti-gun-rights organization. The fledgling group was attempting to organize a media fiesta they had dubbed the Million Mom March. The marchers were a well-funded bunch of women who had a number of Hollywood ties that guaranteed them media access and a steady flow of money.

The five Internet debaters, on the other hand, were just regular people who hailed from New Jersey, Texas, Illinois, South Carolina, and Florida. They agreed the world needed to know the Million Mom Marchers did not speak for them. They quickly formed a group of their own and brilliantly called it the Second Amendment Sisters. In no time at all, with the help of the Internet and without a second glance from standard media outlets, they brought together a large group of like-minded women with the intent of countering the MMM's plan to rally one million anti-rights mothers on the Mall in Washington on Mothers' Day 2000.

In the spring of 2000 I received a call from Mari Thompson, a Texas grandmother and one of the founding Second Amendment Sisters. They were planning a counter-rally on the opposite side of the Mall in D.C. and wanted to know if I would be a guest speaker.

I was thrilled that they had thought of me but, I must admit, was not thrilled at the idea of being in Washington, D.C., on Mothers' Day. I had a four-year-old and a two-year-old at that point, and I knew my husband would not be pleased with my jetting off somewhere away from them on that special day. I think he was sick and tired of having his wife gone, yet again. However, he knew that speaking out against what the Marchers were trying to do was extremely important to me. They could not be allowed to grab all of the media attention without a challenge. We needed anyone watching to know that they did not speak for all of the mothers and grandmothers in this country! We did not dare remain silent for fear that our unwillingness to speak out would be viewed as tacit approval of their views.

With a lump in my throat and a knot in the pit of my stomach, I agreed to fly to D.C. and spend Mothers' Day away from my precious family.

Not being personally endowed with particularly good organizational skills, you can imagine my amazement at the excellent coordination, staging, and attendance at the Second Amendment Sisters inaugural rally on the Mall opposite the MMMs.

I was pleased our team had several top-flight speakers lined up who were far better known than I. I was impressed with the thousands of women and men they had turned out in such a relatively short amount of time and with a fraction of the other side's money.

The weather was very pleasant, so I wore a frilly little dress with a flower pattern on it and pearls. I wanted to look the part of a mother of young children on this special day, instead of a businesswoman or legislator.

In the Enemy Camp

While I had a little free time, I strolled across the grass divide to the enemy's camp. I had been asked to be a guest on the "Today Show," which was being aired live from a simple, cordoned-off tent set up in the midst of the MMMs. I used the minutes I had before my interview to get a feel for the well-meaning women on their side.

I quickly noted how few people there seemed to be in attendance, relative to the hype. To say their numbers fell far short of their projected million would be an understatement. A truer estimate, according to the cops I asked, would have been something between ten and twenty thousand. Of course the marchers did not recognize me as I walked amongst them. Nor did they have any reason to. They had Susan Sarandon, Courtney Love, and other Hollywood hotties on a stage extolling the need for "common sense gun laws."

What I found most interesting was that, while their speakers repeatedly promised they were not trying to take away anyone's guns, nor ban ownership, nearly everyone in the crowd around me proudly wore a button on her chest that stated otherwise. The silhouette of a handgun with a simple red circle around it and a slash through it loudly declared their true desire and intent. It was as if their audience had not gotten the memo.

As the time for my interview neared, I entered the tent area and was briefed on the show plan. Rosie O'Donnell, television show hostess and noted anti-Second Amendment spokeswoman, was to be interviewed by Cokie Roberts. After a commercial break, George Will was to follow with an interview of yours truly.

As I waited in a small area set up for makeup, Rosie O'Donnell walked in with Courtney Love. Love slouched down into a director's chair across from me and looked to be physically ill. She was very pale, with uncombed hair, dark circles around her eyes, and unkempt clothes. In hindsight, I think her appearance may not have been the result of a virus. Very sad. In contrast, Rosie walked right up to me, very politely shook my hand and said, "I'm sorry for your loss." I believe she meant it.

I replied, "Thank you," and she quickly turned on her heels, walked the few steps to the staging area, and sat in a chair opposite Cokie. The interview lasted only a few minutes, and I really wanted to hear every word, but George Will intercepted me. He wisely wanted to do a quick pre-interview with me, so he could have a better feel for what questions he wanted to ask on air. When it came our turn, Mr. Will, who is probably best known for his conservative syndicated newspaper column, asked me several softball questions.

Although I appreciated his kindness, I actually have very mixed feelings about that interview. I have almost come to prefer that the interviewer ask me the really tough questions they are afraid will seem impolite when directed at a "victim." But the questions he did ask were open-ended enough that I was able, I hope, to make some real points.

One of those points I thought was vital was made when he asked about one of the "sensible" gun laws the MMMs wanted regarding firearm registration. They think that it is "only reasonable" to know whose hands the guns are in. Why do I have a problem with that, he asked? Because, I said, registration is always, always, ALWAYS the first step to confiscation. If his audience did not think that was the ultimate goal of these women, then why did nearly everyone on this side of the Mall wear one of those circle/slash buttons, I pointed out.

I got a thrill out of doing that interview from the middle of the enemy's encampment, so to speak. As we finished, I wondered if I would need a bodyguard to walk me back to the other side of the Mall. But beyond a handful of dirty looks I got from onlookers who could hear the interview, no one paid me any mind as I left the area.

Second Amendment Sisters Rally

When I returned to the pro-rights, pro-self-defense side of the Mall, I was fortunate to hear some of the speakers who preceded me on the program. My good friend Neal Knox was there and gave a rousing call to arms that was worthy of the Founders.

Also on the agenda was John Lott. A fascinating man with an economist's mind and a dry wit, John was able to give all of us left-brained types the statistical ammunition we needed to back up our arguments. Like the accidental tourist, this man fell into the heat of the gun debate simply by doing a study on gun-control laws and their connection to crime rates, amidst dozens of other non-gun-related studies in which he was engaged. And then he had the unmitigated gall to tell the press about his findings. As a true academician, he has constantly put his works up for peer review to flesh out any flaws they may find in his study models. They cannot find any, so they resort to attacking him personally and do their very best to shout him down.

But he continues to do yeoman's work.

When it came my turn to take the stage, I recall looking beyond the audience to scan the trees around the Mall perimeter and the streets filled with people. I realized how easy it would be for a lone gunman to be hiding somewhere, me in his sights, ready to do some dirty work for his anti-gun friends with the same stomp-out-violence mentality and rationalization with which abortion clinic bombers delude themselves. It was just a thought, but I could not stop it.

I did my best to let my audience and the press know why I had made the difficult decision to be away from my family on Mothers' Day. I told them my story, despite the occasional microphone feedback and background noise. I did my best to make them feel the pain of not having a mother to spend this special day with, because the law would not let us protect ourselves from a lunatic. While women on the other side of the Mall were clamoring for more gun control, I asked a logical question that went something like this:

"OK, let's see. We had a shooting at a cafeteria in Texas. Oh wait, I must be mistaken. Guns weren't allowed there. Well, then there was that shooting at the post office. Oh no, that couldn't be, there are federal laws against carrying guns into a post office. And don't forget the awful shootings that took place at the Xerox factory in Hawaii. But wait, they had a big 'No Guns' sign—red circle with a slash—at the entrance to their building, so that couldn't have happened. Then there was the Jewish daycare center—do you remember the media images of those innocent little children going across the parking lot hand in hand?—and the schools in Pearl, Mississippi, and Columbine. Hold on a minute, guns aren't allowed in schools.

"Every one of these places where terrible massacres had taken place was a place guns weren't allowed! Does anyone see a pattern here? So if guns are the problem, as the women across the Mall assert, why haven't we seen any of these terrible mass shootings at NRA conventions, or skeet and trap shoots, or the dreaded gun show…places where there are perhaps thousands of guns in the hands of as many law-abiding citizens who believe in their Second Amendment rights? If guns are the problem, someone explain this to me!"

I went on to tell them I had made a stupid decision to obey the law on that October 16th in that Texas restaurant. I told them I would much rather be sitting in jail with a felony offense on my head and have my parents alive to know their grandchildren.

I hoped someone outside the choir was listening. I hoped the press would give us a fair shake.

I returned home feeling I had done my job, and I was grateful to those feisty women who put that amazing rally together. It is always comforting to know there are like-minded people in the world. The so-called Million Mom Marchers did not get a free ride.

The day after Mothers' Day was, of course, Monday, and everybody was back at work. I remember being surprised by a call from my legislative aide who told me Rush Limbaugh was playing sound clips from my Second Amendment Sisters speech and my "Today Show" interview. To say I was surprised would have been an understatement. The words incredulous, amazed, flattered, and humbled come to mind. You could probably even throw in tickled pink.

I was able to catch most of a time-delayed version of his radio talk show an hour later and was more than pleased at how clever he made me sound. Of course, he railed against Rosie. But I was most happy to have some of my comments played to a larger audience that, while conservative, may still contain a few people unsure of the right to self-defense. I also learned from his show that there were numerous news clips of my speech and both rallies being replayed on "CNN Headline News" throughout the day. Good. The more folks who hear both sides, the better, I thought.

CHAPTER 13
The Stupidity
of Gun-Control Laws

Ihave spent a great deal of time pondering some of the words I spoke on that Mothers' Day. I think they are absolutely true. Just as John Lott had asked for peer review of his studies, I have asked for anyone to find the flaws in my logic and enlighten me. To my knowledge, no one has been able to name a mass shooting in this country's recent history that occurred at a location where people were allowed to carry guns. Not one! If there is one, it is obviously so obscure no one can immediately bring it to mind.

I remember watching a short-lived show called "Public Eye" with Bryant Gumbel, in which he interviewed the assistant principal, who brought the terrible school shooting in Pearl, Mississippi, to a halt.

Joel Myrick, assistant principal, Pearl, Mississippi.

If you were a director looking to cast an actor as the assistant principal in that awful event, you could not have done better than that real-life hero, Joel Myrick. He was a well-built, handsome National Guard officer who politely talked circles around the very liberal Gumbel. As he described what happened that morning, his expression betrayed the pain he felt at being unable to protect the many children who were the first victims. Knowing he could not confront the armed assailant with his fists, he ran to the parking lot to retrieve a handgun from his truck.

I saw Gumbel raise his eyebrows slightly. I don't think that was part of his script. Myrick then explained how he stopped the shooter and held him for the police. It was later revealed that the teenage boy had already stabbed his mother to death before proceeding to the school, where he shot two girls to death and wounded seven other students. There is no telling what the body count would have been had it not been for that brave, committed assistant principal and his own handgun.

Now I am pretty sure his gun was kept on school grounds illegally, and I am completely sure that Gumbel did not know the story was going to go that way. I was screaming at the television set to make those points. But of course, Gumbel quietly sloughed over it in his very professional-sounding but incomplete way.

Another dreadful school shooting took place in the cafeteria at a high school in Springfield, Oregon, but the carnage was stopped when several students rushed and overpowered the evildoer. Seventeen-year-old Jake Ryker, who waited until the shooter's gun was empty and had to be reloaded, led them. Ryker didn't realize it when he made his move, but he had already been hit in the chest by a bullet that broke a rib and went through his right lung. When he charged, his fourteen-year-old brother Josh and several other students backed him up.

I met and spoke with one of the Ryker boys and his proud, but shaken, father. The boy's first-hand account would send a chill up any parent's spine. As hunters and shooters themselves, the Rykers and several other students in the cafeteria were familiar with rifles, the type of weapon the murderer was using. They realized by the click when the gun was empty. Those incredibly brave

*Jake Ryker, student,
Springfield, Oregon.*

young heroes rushed the demented student who was bent on so much destruction.

When Jake Ryker hit the shooter with a wrestling tackle, it sent the semi-automatic rifle flying. But the killer pulled a 9 mm pistol, and in the struggle it discharged, sending another bullet through Ryker's left index finger. In choosing to fight back, those students saved an untold number of lives. My heart swells with pride for those boys.

When a couple of them were being interviewed by a news anchor who wanted to turn the spotlight on the gun laws, these boys surprised him by speaking of the guns they personally owned and how their knowledge brought the gunman down.

The Shootings Continued

Some time later there was a shooting at Appalachian University School of Law where two students who ran to their vehicles and retrieved firearms of their own abruptly stopped the perpetrator. You just didn't hear very much from the mainstream media about how that disaster was thwarted. What would the body-bag count have been, were it not for those courageous law students and their guns?

More recently was the Virginia Tech massacre, which now holds the record—a dubious honor—for largest number of casualties. Thirty-two people were killed at Tech, and the shooter committed suicide, bringing the total to thirty-three. That horrific episode dwarfed the previous record of twenty-three set at Luby's cafeteria in 1991.

As I read the headlines the next morning, I could not help but think there was some sicko somewhere else reading it also and thinking, "thirty-two? I could shoot more than that!" It is a hard thing to grasp, but I am quite certain people exist who are merely a tick away from proving their insanity. Where are they going to go to get that high body-bag count? I do not think it will be a gun show, skeet and trap shoot, or NRA convention. I do not think it will be in a restaurant or other business where concealed-carry is allowed. They want to go where they can rack up the numbers. They want to go where it is easy pickin's, like shooting fish in a barrel.

Yet, many people still insist we should "let the policemen do their job. They will protect you." The naïveté of such a remark is striking. In April 2009 in Binghamton, New York, a gunman entered a civic association center that caters to immigrants and opened fire on a room full of people taking a citizenship class. One receptionist was shot in the abdomen, but was able to dial 9-1-1 for help, while the killer moved on to murder thirteen others and then commit suicide. The police arrived within two minutes. Admirable. But then, according to an Associated Press article dated April 3, 2009, they "waited for about an hour before entering the building to make sure it was safe for officers." Let me repeat that: *the police arrived two minutes after the shooting began, but did not enter the building for an hour.* How many victims bled to death during that time? Did that innocent, brave, gut-shot woman that made the call survive? The article did not say.

That dreadful example is not an anomaly. Some said it took nearly an hour for officers to finally enter Columbine High School out of fear of potential booby traps. I do not blame the police forces. They must keep their officers safe.

I only bring this to your attention to instill an understanding of the need to take responsibility for your own safety. As my prosecutor friend had once declared, the police are usually just the clean-up crew. It's true, but disturbing.

Like Sheep to a Slaughter

The anti-gun crowd is leading the victims to these killers like sheep to a slaughter. You read me right. For now, after the last twenty years of multiple murder-suicides, how could anyone in their right mind believe otherwise? By labeling certain places "Gun-Free Zones," what they have actually done is unwittingly create something that wackos translate into "Target-Rich Environment" or "Defenseless Sheep: Kill Here."

For years I have used that argument with my legislative friends and any reporter who would listen. I filed a bill numerous times that would have allowed concealed-carry on university properties in Texas, but could not get it through the entire system. In making my argument, I wanted to get accurate statistics regarding on-campus, violent crime. But university officials who did not want that information to get out thwarted my efforts at every turn. After all, if you knew how many rapes, robberies, assaults, or murders really occur on our university grounds, there is a pretty good chance you would not spend money to send your kids there! They have separate police departments, and even as a legislator I could not pry the information out of them. I began to believe the rumors I had heard from students about rampant campus crime.

Think how just the knowledge that someone — or more than one — may be legally armed and could shoot back would prevent these nut jobs from taking that final step. In the case of these guys who are going for a high body count, yes, it is likely they could kill a few people. But they sure as heck would not get thirty-two before they were taken out of action.

How glorious it would have been if that gentleman who was a professor and holocaust survivor at Tech could have done more than just block the door. Do you think he would have hesitated to pull a trigger and end the carnage? No way. There was a man who clearly knew that evil exists in this world. He had already suffered at the hands of his government. He survived the Holocaust, but he could not survive the laws passed by the Virginia State Legislature. How ironic and incredibly tragic.

A Personal Story

With a far less drastic outcome, my husband and I had already experienced the unfairness of laws that prevent concealed-carry on university campuses. Several years ago, Greg was an adjunct professor at a campus where he was completing his doctorate in psychology. There were many evenings when he was there well beyond the time when most students had gone home. I was concerned about him, and was not about to lose my husband to violence the way I had lost my parents. So I insisted that he carry a handgun and not make the same mistake I had made a few years earlier by obeying a dangerous law.

One evening, as he made his way through a mostly deserted parking lot, two young guys in a little car zipped around by his pickup and tossed a bottle into the truck's bed. As they parked their car a few spots away, Greg reached into the back of his truck, retrieved the bottle, and walked to the car where they still sat. Their window was down, so my husband said, "I think you dropped this."

To which the driver of the little car said in classic bully style, "So what are you going to do about it?"

At that point, Greg said, "I just wanted to make sure you got it back." As he said it, he dropped the bottle onto the floor behind the driver's seat and turned to go. The student threw open the door, attacked Greg from behind, and with the martial arts training we later found out he had received at the university put my six-foot two-inch husband face down on the pavement with a foot at the back of his neck.

As the hard ground flew up to meet him, Greg was barely able to get his hand on the little gun he kept in his pocket and withdraw it. He was not sure what the thug said at that moment. The wind had been knocked out of him so hard he was gasping for air. But the guy did remove his foot, and Greg heard the thug's friend cry, "He's got a gun! Let's get out of here." Both quickly retreated, jumped in their little car, and sped from the parking lot.

Of course, Greg could not risk reporting the assault, because he was carrying the gun illegally. Other than a few bruises, he thought that was the end of it. To his amazement and without my immediate knowledge, he was asked to come to the campus police department a few days later to "answer a few questions." Incredibly, the two students whose asinine behavior had triggered the whole event had reported the incident.

The investigating cop needed Greg's side of the story. Here is where my husband made a mistake. In this country, most of us who are raised decently are taught to tell the truth: if you are innocent, justice will prevail. Maybe I am just more cynical, but if I had been telling Greg's side of the story, I would have left out the part about the gun. No need to incriminate oneself. Then it becomes their word against yours.

Unfortunately, my husband still believed in justice and his own innocence. He told the whole truth. The cop shook his head and said, "Well, that's pretty much what they told me…which I don't understand, since they confessed to an assault. But we're going to have to charge you with a weapons violation."

They got slapped with Class B misdemeanors. My husband, the victim in the whole scenario, was given deferred adjudication for a Class A misdemeanor. I really wanted to take it to a jury, but our crummy attorney talked us out of it, saying it would cost us twice as much and came with no guarantees. We did not have the money to risk.

It is a shame when you have to pay for justice to be served. It cost us thousands of dollars to walk away with one year's probation and community service. For a time, we did not know if the Class A would prevent him from receiving the doctorate he had spent so much money, and so many years, trying to achieve. The *coup de gras* was that our concealed-carry law passed shortly afterward, and the violation prevented him from being eligible for a permit for five years.

We had been sucker punched. What kind of a government punishes people for protecting themselves?

It's Beyond Ironic

We live close to the largest military installation in the free world: Fort Hood. As a state legislator, it was my honor to represent a large number of those soldiers and their families. Many times I have been approached by eighteen-, nineteen-, and twenty-year-old active duty military personnel, who were frustrated by a system that prevented them from getting a concealed-carry permit until their twenty-first birthday. To paraphrase them, they thought it was "nuts" to send them overseas with a gun in their hands to protect our country and the freedoms we all enjoy, only to bring them home and tell them, essentially, it was not all right for them to defend themselves and their young families from homebred criminals.

It went beyond "ironic." It sent the morale-busting message that our government did not trust them. They put their lives on the line for all of us, yet they were denied the very rights inherent in the Constitution they fought to protect! "Nuts" did not begin to cover how insane that was.

Over the past several years, I made numerous attempts to correct that situation in the state of Texas. At the very least, I reasoned, we should lower the age limit on concealed-carry permits to eighteen for active-duty military personnel. The nonsensical argument I have always gotten in return is the same one used to keep the minimum drinking age at twenty-one: eighteen-, nineteen-, and twenty-year-olds are old enough to die for our country, but not old enough to act responsibly here at home.

The Texas legislature has recently corrected this inane situation. Veterans and active-duty military personnel can qualify for a concealed-handgun license at the age of eighteen. However, this is not the case in many other states. It is amazing we haven't seen a revolt!

I constantly worry about the children of our active-duty military, as well. Just as elementary schools in Israel were a target of terrorists for many years, I wonder when those evildoers will begin to prey upon the innocent children of our soldiers. It is a sickening thought, but one that has come to fruition in other countries many times. Remember the Russian school massacre that occurred at Beslan in 2004? Over three hundred civilians were killed, one hundred eighty-six of whom were little children.

That end came only after three days of pure hell for the hostages. Officials tried to negotiate for drinking water to be delivered in the hope they could ease the hostages' suffering and possibly prevent deaths from dehydration. But those innocents were allowed no water. And kindergarteners were forced to drink urine from their own tiny shoes in order to survive. The bloodshed, brutality, and pure evil to which they were subjected for three interminable days will affect the survivors for an eternity.

It was later said that the terrorists laughed at the babies' misery and pain. All the while, there were parents waiting on the outside for three days, not knowing their children's fate, but hearing rumors of the ongoing torture. I cannot fathom the absolute agony and feelings of impotence they must have endured at the hands of men and women so determined to alter their own little worlds through the most horrific means possible.

I am not aware of any of the adults inside that school having weapons. It is my understanding that they, like us, were not allowed to carry concealed or otherwise for their own and their students' protection. They, too, were under that false belief that carrying a weapon is just unseemly in a civilized country. What an unbearable way to learn otherwise. I simply cannot imagine a more cruel eye-opener.

Are we Americans any different? What would stop such a horrific event from occurring here? It pains me that I can think of nothing. The terrorists would love nothing more than to inflict such a wound upon us. If not political terrorists, what about the occasional nut job right in your own neighborhood who is plotting, in his worm-infested mind, how to get a higher body-bag count and capture the headlines?

Are Our Teachers Second-Class Citizens?

I do not want to put great walls around our schools with armed guards in towers at each corner. I do not want to have to present easily falsified identification at the entrance or march through a metal detector. I do not want my children taught it is OK for them to be subjected to random searches of their belongings. Sure, such searches will occasionally turn up illegal drugs or evidence of some petty crime. But our children will be living in a prison, with daily reminders of their vulnerability.

I reject that un-American scenario with every fiber of my being.

I want to know why my teachers are being treated like second-class citizens? I can protect myself on the job. Lawyers, doctors, engineers, plumbers, and even legislators can protect themselves on the job. So why don't we trust our teachers?

Well Suzanna, you might say, *some of them are in high-stress situations where they might just lose it some day. We do not want that teacher to have easy access to a firearm!*

What is to keep that from happening now?

Well at our school, Suzanna, they have to go through the same metal detector as the kids.

Big deal. If they are planning to kill kids, what is to keep them from blasting the guard at the metal detector first, then moving on to their favorite classroom, while the metal detector beeps away?

In my opinion, teachers are no different from the rest of society. There are good ones, bad ones, sweet ones, angelic ones, and an occasional sadistic fiend thrown in as well. Unfortunately, we cannot usually sort them apart or recognize them by sight. We do know this: evildoers are much more likely to hold themselves in check when they know there is a chance of dying in the process of acting out their sickness.

On the unusual occasion when a twisted-minded maniac does not value his own life and, in fact, desires to take a large number of victims with him on his suicidal mission, he will look elsewhere to commit his crime, out of fear he won't be able to complete it in any spectacular fashion. He will not know who else is armed or who will prevent him from continuing his murderous rampage.

I have heard many arguments against concealed-carry in schools that seem to center on the concept of teachers not being trained as policemen. But we are not talking about giving them power to arrest or a vast knowledge of various felonies and misdemeanors. We are talking about a last line of defense between a homicidal maniac and themselves and possibly the children in their care. I wonder when the teachers' groups will figure out they are being treated as inferiors and suspect!

While I was in the legislature, two superintendents from a couple of really rural school districts came to me with a small request: they wanted me to pass a bill that would give them the ability to carry a concealed weapon on campus. Now when I say rural, I am talking about one traffic light in the entire county. Rural. They were contending with an ugly little cottage industry that had sprung up in their county in which people were taking in foster care children and receiving some pretty good money—compared to no income at all—from the state in return.

Now, a lot of people move out to the country to escape the problems of city life. But in this particular county a large number of those children who had been snatched from their birth families in inner-city Dallas or Houston, sometimes for good reason, sometimes not, had been deposited in these small communities. Some were good kids, but many brought the crime and gang problems they had grown up with in the city out to the country...and to the tiny school systems that did their best to welcome them with open arms.

These superintendents were concerned. They simply were not equipped to handle some of the problems that came with those children and teenagers, and there was no way the towns or county were going to provide them with full-time peace officers of their own. They claimed there had recently been one particularly nasty incident, details of which were not shared, as there was a trial pending, in which the sheriff's office took forty-five minutes to respond. That was not due to anything out of the ordinary. The deputy just happened to be at the other end of the county. Not unusual at all.

Their very legitimate concern was that, in the wake of Columbine and having several students of their own who were known to be unstable, it would be up to them to stop any murderous tirade that might occur on their campuses. They were also savvy enough to know that getting a law passed enabling their teachers to carry was an unattainable goal at present.

After some discussion, I had a bill drafted and filed that would allow superintendents in low-population counties to carry concealed weapons. Certainly I believe any school official should be able to carry, but I felt by limiting it to superintendents in rural counties, our chances of getting it passed were far greater.

We did get a hearing, and it received national attention. However, I let the bill quietly die after the arguments had been made. You see, in fleshing out the wording, we discovered a little glitch in the current law we all felt would take care of their problem. The statute stated that the head of a school could give written permission for someone to carry a gun on campus. It was very poorly worded, for none of us knew who the "head" of a school was. Does that mean the school-board president, principal, or superintendent?

Behind closed doors, my constituents and I decided it was in their students' and their own best interests to quietly give themselves written permission and go ahead and carry. We ascertained that in the best-case scenario, no one would know they were carrying a gun—it would be concealed, after all. In the worst-case scenario, they would have the ability to save lives. No prosecutor in that part of the state would be silly enough to go after them.

In August 2008, the news media heard about a change of policy in one small Texas school district. Harrold School District would allow qualified teachers to carry concealed handguns in the district's single school. The teachers would be required to have a Texas concealed-handgun license, receive training in crisis management and hostile situations, and use ammunition that was designed not to ricochet. The school is about 150 miles northwest of Fort Worth, close to the Oklahoma border. It has 110 students and is a thirty-minute drive from the sheriff's office. Harrold was the first school district in the nation to adopt such a policy, according to news reports.

❖ ❖ ❖

CHAPTER 14
Speaking Out:
from Washington to Hawaii

Some time after the Million Mom March, or as I like to call it, the Second Amendment Sisters Rally, I was invited to be part of an episode of "Good Morning America" that would air from the White House. I knew I would be walking into a hornet's nest, and I was likely to be significantly outnumbered, but I still felt obligated to be part of the battle. It turned out I was correct in my assumptions. Of the fifteen or so who were to be part of the show, it quickly became evident that only three or four of us actually believed in protecting the Second Amendment.

Once we were ushered into our seating area, President Bill Clinton entered the room and took a place at the front. He did his best to look concerned. When a few other guests told stories of how their loved ones became the victims of a gun—not the bad guy or their own suicidal tendencies, but the gun—the producers concurrently ran videotape of any news broadcasts they had of that event.

When it was my turn to tell a story from a little different viewpoint, for some interesting reason, the news videos of the Luby's incident just would not play. They apologized for the technical problem. Hmmm. I was given only a moment to direct a comment to the President, and I did not want to appear blatantly rude by just yelling stuff across the small group. It was very frustrating. While I respected the office, I did not respect the man. I exhibited decorum, nonetheless.

Also present was the actress and NRA board member, Susan Howard, who was absolutely brilliant. She politely, but adroitly, excoriated Clinton in such a way that he could not completely recover before the show ended. It was beautiful.

When the show was completed, President Clinton stayed in the room long enough to shake hands and pose for photos with the guests. I briefly considered it—he was the President, after all—and I argued back and forth with myself in silence for several minutes. In the end, I could not help wondering if the hand he was using to greet the women in the room was the same hand that had held the infamous cigar. A disgusting thought, I know. But I just couldn't shake it—the thought or his hand.

So many women in that room believed, deep down in their souls, that guns animate themselves on a regular basis and shoot children. You have all heard the various statistics that lead you to think that little children die every day from accidentally getting hold of Daddy's gun.

The real truth behind those statistics was made clear to me when I testified before a notoriously anti-gun legislative committee in Hawaii. They knew I had been flown in for the hearing at the significant expense of the local rifle association. As the starting time neared, the committee had well over a hundred witness forms from residents wishing to testify. The chairman called the meeting to order and announced he would take witnesses in alternating order. In other words, he would have one speak for the bill and then one against the bill. Of course, that would not have lasted long due to the large difference in the number of pro versus con witnesses.

The legislation was introduced and the first witness was called. This guy was against any pro-gun legislation you could have come up with, and he was allowed to testify for forty-five minutes. The second witness was Gary Kleck, a Florida State University criminologist and self-proclaimed liberal. But in doing his research, he discovered that guns are used to prevent crimes far more often than they are used to commit crimes. In interviewing felons, he found they were far more worried about confronting an armed citizen than they were about the police. He made a superb witness, but they let him speak for only fifteen minutes before the chairman cut him off. From that point on, the chairman declared, witnesses would have only two minutes to make their points.

One more anti-gun witness spoke, and then it was my turn. I quickly told them what they already knew: I was an invited guest and had been flown in for this occasion. I politely asked for eight minutes to give my testimony. He basically said, "Tough, you have two minutes." Members of the audience yelled out they would give up their time to me. He repeated, "You have two minutes," and added, "The clock has been started."

It was his committee, and he got to make the rules. Having been a committee chairman myself, during highly volatile hearings, I understand the occasional necessity for limiting witness testimony. But, when you know that someone has been flown in at great expense, and other witnesses are willing to transfer their time, it is hard to believe his decision was out of anything more than belligerence. Anyway, I did my best to tell my story briefly.

Then I went outside and told the whole story to those who really counted: the press. Although the committee did not hear my testimony that day, they, and their constituents, read it in its entirety in the next day's newspaper.

When I reentered the auditorium, a man was speaking who got my immediate attention. He had a stack of files in front of him that had been used in compiling the childhood firearm deaths statistics. In reviewing them, he was surprised to find out that, for the study, "childhood" included eighteen-, nineteen-, twenty-, and even twenty-one-year olds. Looking at it more closely, eight- or nine-year-olds accidently getting their hands on a gun and killing a friend or family member was not the norm—it was rare.

He began to flip through the files and read the summaries aloud. One after the other, it was "drug deal gone bad, drug deal gone bad, gang member killing rival, drug deal gone bad." And an overwhelming percentage of these "children" were seventeen and older.

That certainly is not to say that accidents don't happen. But they should be treated as such. If there is gross negligence involved, that should be considered as well. However, it became quite clear that the public has been largely misled on the subject and, to this day, continues to be led down a dead-end path by the anti-Second Amendment crowd.

The Employee Parking Lot Conundrum

Another odd conundrum has been coming up before various state legislatures of late. Bills are being drafted to keep employers from reprimanding or firing employees who leave firearms in their own cars on the workplace parking lot. I initially had some mixed feelings about this subject, which I think surprised a lot of people. But, you see, I believe in private property rights as strongly as I believe in our Second Amendment. Simplistically, if your employer makes stupid rules, you have the right to quit. Whoever owns the business makes the rules. But of course, there is more to it than that.

Here is the conclusion I believe to be consistent with both sets of rights: if a business owner has an "employees only" parking lot that prevents public access, then he has the right to say who and what can enter, and the employee can park elsewhere. Conversely, if the lot where the employees park also invites the public to enter into it (and thereby people with carry permits or hunting weapons) — for example, a gas station or Wal-Mart — the employer/ owner must not discriminate against the employees.

I believe one more distinction should be made that was clarified for me by a caller to a radio talk show I hosted: if the business receives government funding, i.e., taxpayer money, they should not be allowed to prevent their employees from exercising their Second Amendment rights. I thought it was an excellent point!

But business owners beware! Included in any new laws should be a provision clearly stating that *the employer takes on the responsibility and the liability for the lives of employees to whom he has denied the right of self-protection*. By stripping away their ability to protect themselves, the business owner must assume the role of Protector and all of the baggage that goes with it. It would be only a matter of time before an injured employee or the family of a murdered employee would file a lawsuit in that regard, and I would be cheering for them.

CHAPTER 15
Abuse of the Fourth Amendment

I'm going to switch gears a little bit. For many years, even before my parents were killed, I have been frustrated by the encroachment upon my Fourth Amendment rights involving unlawful searches. Did I mention that I like all ten of the amendments in our Bill of Rights?

There have been times I have purchased tickets to concerts, at venues both large and small, only to be surprised by a "pop" inspection of my purse at the door by some minimum-wage worker with a red vest and name tag. Dad used to tell me that the ticket constituted a contract, and it did not say anything about subjecting myself or my belongings to a search.

I do not know how correct he was, or how legally binding that "contract" really was, but I never had the guts to make an issue of it. You know how it is: you are usually there with friends, who may not be quite as passionate about our rights as you are, and they may just wait until after the show to bail you out of jail.

But having some stranger rifle through my belongings, without probable cause, has always offended me; particularly when these so-called searches are so markedly lame. Several times my husband or I have carried concealed into an area where "the management" did not allow it. But there are four times, in particular, that stand out as examples of this inane and bothersome routine.

The first one occurred several years ago, before Greg and I were married. A married couple we knew invited us to attend a big Austin street festival. Every year the city fathers close off a couple of the streets in downtown Austin and fill them with vendors and street bands and lots and lots of people. It was not a good place to carry a purse. So I put my gun into a fanny pack that was designed with that purpose in mind.

The pistol is held with Velcro in a hidden compartment next to your body, and my identification, money, and lipstick went in the main compartments in front of the gun. Late in the evening, they began funneling those of us who had bought tickets for a street dance into a roped-off section. It was very loud and very crowded, and it would have been easy to lose track of one another.

As we got closer to the end of the funnel, we could hear our friend politely arguing with a female cop who stood at the head of the line he and his wife were in, but could not catch the content of the discussion. Then my attention was suddenly brought back to my line, where a police officer was standing with flashlight in hand, blocking my final entrance to the dance and demanding that I open my fanny pack.

Once again, although the hair on the back of my neck stood up at his intrusion, we were with friends, and I did not want to spoil the night. On the other hand, that was also before concealed-carry was legal in this state, so I was definitely breaking the law. I took a chance and jerked open the obvious front compartment of my pack. The officer shined his flashlight into it, then waved me on, oblivious to the .38 revolver held snugly a quarter inch behind the lipstick.

We moved into the crowded dance area, and our friends came forward quickly from their own line and abruptly pushed us into the dark mass of moving people. When we were some distance from the police, our friend told us that the female cop with whom he was arguing wanted to confiscate the enormous knife that he carried attached to his key chain. Initially, he thought she was joking, but she was quite serious, and he was not going to give up his keepsake so easily. She made the mistake of turning away from him for a few moments and, with the noise, darkness, and confusion all around them, he took the advantage and bolted.

Should you think that I have slimy friends who get in trouble with the law on a routine basis, let me provide reassurance to the contrary. My friend was a doctor, and the pocketknife the policewoman was so concerned about had a one-inch blade. Lord knows how many people he could have butchered with that little letter opener.

After he showed us the cause of the hullabaloo, I discretely opened the rear compartment of my pack, briefly exposing the contents to him. I had barely been inconvenienced for ten seconds for my illegally carried deadly weapon, while he had been forced to dodge the law in order to hold onto his tiny camping trip souvenir.

Searching V.I.P.s at the Capitol

A second significant time my Fourth Amendment rights were infringed upon without due cause occurred a few years after the Texas concealed-carry law was enacted. I was a member of the legislature, and a big stage was set up in front of the Texas Capitol for Governor George W. Bush to make his presidential election night acceptance speech. (Of course, that speech got hung up on some chads in Florida for several weeks.)

Greg and I did not want to miss the historic event. So my husband and I walked from my reserved parking place on the Capitol grounds, with my purse and its contents legally in hand, only to be met by another Representative heading the opposite direction. Knowing of my propensity to carry a weapon, he told us that the Secret Service had closed off part of the street up ahead and were funneling even us invited-types through a metal detector. My friend was also legally carrying and did not want the hassle.

He kindly agreed to take my gun back to his Capitol office with him. So, after a quick debate of our options, I handed my little revolver over to my fellow Representative.

We continued on toward the metal detectors, where I was asked to hand my purse around to an agent while I walked through the device. In typical fashion, the agent opened the main compartment of my handbag, glanced inside, shuffled the contents around in an embarrassed manner, and handed it back to me. Good grief, that ticked me off! If you are going to do it, do it right!

When it happened a second time upon entering a cordoned off building just a few moments later, I couldn't stand it anymore. I asked to see the agent in charge, and visually filled him in on his agents' errors by opening the side pocket of my purse and exposing the empty holster. I was not sure that he appreciated my corrections, but I was very polite, and went on to ask him a few more questions that he probably did not appreciate.

I genuinely wanted to know what statute gave them the ability to shut down a public road—remember, Bush was not President yet—and prevent me from lawfully carrying my firearm. I was OK with their checkpoints—sort of—but how and why would they keep those of us with concealed-carry permits from carrying our weapons? Of course, he could not give me a sufficient answer, and I did not press for one.

A Fourth of July Search

A third time that my Fourth Amendment rights were violated in a significant way occurred at a rather embarrassing place. As the State Legislator representing part of their base, Fort Hood always invited Greg and me to attend their Fourth of July festivities. You haven't lived until you experience a Fourth of July celebration on a large military base, surrounded by people who walk the walk. It stands as one of the most inspirational and patriotic experiences of my life.

In previous years, we had been given V.I.P. status for parking and seating, which only added to a glorious and enjoyable evening. But on July 4th, 2002, what had previously been an open base was now closed as a result of 9/11, and many serious precautions were being taken. So, it came as no surprise when we were asked to park in a remote location and board a shuttle bus that would take us a mile or so to the grandstand.

When we disembarked, however, we were shocked to find ourselves standing in a line where even the V.I.P.s were being subjected to a search! I do not mean that they were putting on rubber gloves and asking us to grab our ankles, but the MPs were definitely patting people down and looking in purses. I was thankful I had decided to leave my purse back in the car, but Greg was another story. He pointed to the metal clip holding his tiny .22 caliber to the inside of his pants pocket. We were in a dilemma. It was too far back to the car for Greg to stash his weapon, and I was fairly sure that even if we were caught, the General in charge would let us pass. But I was not certain.

At that moment, another shuttle emptied its passengers into the crowded little tent where people were filing past the MPs. Greg instantly decided to take a chance. The upshot of the story is that, as my eight-year-old niece's bag full of Aquafina bottles was being searched, my husband walked right on through. As a side note, later that evening I saw an ambulance—you know, a big truck that could carry lots of explosives—waved through a line of cars that was being checked for bombs. That could have been a very bad decision.

So Much for Security

The fourth time occurred a couple of weeks after the 9/11 attacks. It was late September, and I was slated to speak to a large group of pro-gun folks in New York. Airlines had just begun flying again, and I really did not want to get on a commercial jet. I tried my best to graciously get out of the speaking engagement, but they insisted that I come. Of course, at that time, the airlines and airport security were very jumpy and would not even let nail clippers on board a plane.

No one was very clear on the new rules, so I entered the secured area with my usual purse and baggage contents. To my amazement, I made it on board with five temporarily illegal items: three one-inch blade pocket knives — lobby gimmes — one long pair of tweezers, and a five-inch, pointed metal nail file. On my return flight, a security guard found one of the items. So much for airport security.

I recall the old "All In The Family" series in which the Archie Bunker character voiced his solution to the airplane-hijacking problem of his day. He said something like, "The stewardess ought to be standing at the door of the plane handing out a gun to every passenger as they board, see? That'll make those hijackers think twice!" Point well made, Archie.

Those four incidents helped me draw this conclusion: the results of half-baked, poorly run searches are not worth usurping our Fourth Amendment rights for the perception of security.

Not Allowed to Shoot

Some of the ridiculous differences in how various states regard our gun rights were driven home to me during that New York trip. Shortly before giving my speech to over a thousand gun owners and their families, the group allowed for a meet-and-greet between the audience members and the speakers, many of whom had already addressed the crowd. John Lott was seated to my left and was autographing several copies of his most recent book for grateful fans. Oddly, when he finished penning his name, several of them stepped forward and requested a note from me on it as well. As I told John, it was very awkward signing someone else's book.

One gentleman came forward with his eleven-year-old son, and they introduced themselves. The young boy was well dressed and conducted himself as an adult. I made some small talk with them and asked the obvious question of the boy, "So, do you go shooting?"

He said, "No. I'm not allowed to shoot."

I looked briefly up at the father, but directed my next question to the boy, "What do you mean, you're 'not allowed to shoot'?"

"I'm only eleven, and in New York I can't shoot until I'm twelve."

I asked, "You mean they won't allow you to shoot on public shooting ranges?"

Seeing my confusion, his dad finally stepped in and explained to me that the New York state law made it illegal for anyone under twelve to shoot a gun on public or private property.

I could not believe my ears. How on earth had we gotten to the point that lawmakers can tell parents what their kids can and cannot do on private property? Assuming there is no abuse, neglect, or reckless endangerment, what part of the Constitution gives them such power? I was flabbergasted.

Minutes later, it was my turn to give my speech. Of course, I had a previously prepared outline of what I wanted to say, but I was still in shock over what the boy and his dad had shared with me. So I began my speech with a recount of the conversation that had just taken place. Then I followed with a slightly different story of what I had witnessed less than twenty-four hours earlier in Oklahoma.

The Other End of the Spectrum

The night before I had been the keynote speaker for the Oklahoma State Rifle Association's annual banquet. They were a much smaller group than the one I was currently addressing, but no less dedicated. I had arrived at the host hotel a bit earlier than planned, so an association member showed me around the meeting rooms.

As we walked down a long hall, he pointed out the various mini-seminars that were being conducted. We passed by one small room that had an open door, and he mentioned that it was the nursery for people who wanted to attend meetings, but needed a place to park their kids. I glanced in and continued on…for about two steps. Then I backed up and did a classic double take. It was a small room that was busy with activity. Closest to me were several toddlers with building blocks and other toys. But what had caught my attention was what was going on at the far end of the room.

Two or three adults had a long table set up about ten feet from the back wall. Hanging from the ceiling and about six inches from that wall was a double thickness of remnant carpeting. Mounted on the carpet were several small paper targets. To my further amazement, there were several very small children with BB guns receiving instruction from the adults across the table from them. This was the nursery? I was quite impressed that the hotel even allowed the activity.

After my speech at the Oklahoma banquet that same evening, the president of the club began drawing tickets for door prizes. One of the first tickets they called belonged to a five- or six-year-old boy who walked from the back of the room to receive his booty. To his and my surprise, they handed him a brand new Red Rider BB gun, still in the box. This kid was so little, as he held one end of the box under his arm, the back end actually dragged on the ground as he toddled back to his table.

I learned later that it is the club's custom to surprise children who are first-timers to the banquet with a BB gun. Upon their second year, they receive a pair of binoculars. I could not help but laugh; if only Diane Feinstein could see this!

It was the next morning that I flew to New York and had my conversation with the eleven-year-old and his father. In less than twenty-four hours, I had witnessed two opposite ends of the gun-culture spectrum. It was hard to comprehend that these two states were within the same country and under the same Constitution.

Note: The text of the Bill of Rights and Al Gratia's letter to an El Paso newspaper regarding the Fourth Amendment appear as Appendices.

CHAPTER 16
More Interviews

I have done hundreds of interviews over the years following that dreadful incident at the Luby's cafeteria. In fact, you name the show, newspaper, or magazine, and I have probably been a guest on it or quoted in it. The experiences I have had with media folk range from downright painful, to amusing, and even to uncomfortably flattering.

In 2004, I was asked to be on Penn and Teller's Showtime show called "Bulls--t!" (Sorry if that offends anyone, but I didn't name it.) I had not seen the show, but the producer explained to me that in each episode, a commonly held belief was effectively shredded by the co-hosts in a humorous but logic-based fashion.

Normally I would never consent to reducing such an important and personally painful topic to comic production. But I had seen the magician/comedic duo of Penn Jillette and Raymond Teller on other television shows over the years, and I knew that their views were very libertarian. I threw caution to the wind and agreed to do the show, with one tiny little caveat: I wanted some of the filming to occur during a raffle with which I was involved.

This wasn't just any raffle. This was the culmination of the efforts of a few mothers, myself included, who wanted to supply the funds for a fence to be built around our intermediate school. There had been a few incidents in which kids were approached by unknowns while away from the main building, but still on the school grounds. Some wise member of the Parent-Teacher-Student Organization checked the Internet and discovered that a number of registered sex offenders lived within a few blocks of the campus.

It was determined that a fence between the sidewalk where kids jogged during physical education classes and the road might be a good idea. Although I was not a member of the PTSO, I ate breakfast with several of the ladies each Monday morning at the Country Kitchen and joined in their discussions.

Marta Ellison and Sharon Fehmel worked hard at raising money for all kinds of school projects, and it always pained me a little to sit back and watch. I just could not bring myself to join in most of the activities, although Greg and I nearly always bought some cookie dough, Christmas wreaths, cheap jewelry, or whatever other items were being pushed "for the kids." I used to beg them to let us write a check at the beginning of the school year that would get us off the hook for the ten months of little bites.

So one Monday morning in autumn, when the conversation revolved around fundraising, I mentioned how nice it would be for them to make fewer sales for more money. We also knew it wouldn't be too many weeks before the Kitchen would be filled to the brim with hunters, in town for the opening of whitetail season. It was a big deal in our town. Banners were strung across the four-lane main street, while a local bank and grocery store partnered to welcome visitors to town with breakfast barbecue. Wouldn't it be nice of us to let those out-of-towners contribute to our fence project? And what would a hunter buy? Well, how about raffle tickets for a chance at a Kimber deer rifle with a Leupold scope?

Voilà! A fundraiser was born!

The idea was not particularly original. I had seen gun raffles used as building fundraisers for other schools. But the media, nonetheless, had a feeding frenzy. There were stories printed and tickets sold all across the nation, as well as Canada, Scotland, and England. Over ten thousand chances were sold, and more than a few went to camo-wearing men and women at the café. The attention it received was not a surprise to me at all, but I am afraid it came as a bit of an unwelcome shock to some of the town-folk, although most seemed to take it in stride.

I think a lot of people just had fun saying "rifle raffle" over and over really fast. Since the idea was hatched in the popular diner, we decided it would be the perfect place to have the final drawing. Mayor Jack Calvert agreed to do the honors, even though he knew that the film crew for "Bulls--t!" would be there. I thought that was pretty gutsy of him.

My legislative colleague, friend, and avid hunter Carl Isett won the second prize of a slightly less expensive rifle. But the winner of the Grand Prize could not have been scripted into the part more perfectly. It turned out to be a local substitute teacher, who had planned to hunt for the first time that year and whose daughter attended the school that the fundraiser would benefit. She was actually teaching when her ticket was drawn, but someone quickly got her there to claim her prize and fifteen minutes of fame.

During a lull in the festivities, I heard someone mention that the Kimber rifle with its Leupold sights might be more effective than a fence for keeping the sex offenders at bay. Hmmm.

When the show finished taping and finally aired, my intuition proved to be right. The hosts concluded it was the gun-control laws that were "Bulls--t!" But in the process, while the tape showed me strolling in front of my horses clad in jeans and a knit sweater, Penn actually said I was "hot, for a legislator." I am not quite sure if that was a compliment or a slap in the face. But, as you can imagine, my friends and husband took great delight in teasing me about it for weeks.

In the spring of 2000, Peter Jennings and ABC's "World News Tonight" contacted me to do a segment on the gun-control debate. Or so I thought. When it aired on Friday, May 5th, just a week before the over-hyped Million Mom

March, I was surprised and more than a little humbled to hear the lead in: apparently they were inaugurating a new feature called "A 21st Century Life." Jennings indicated that they were bombarded by a number of emails suggesting me for their first show. I am still not clear how that came about.

It ended up being a positive piece that, at first glance, could have been put together by my campaign staff. There were several clips of me in jeans with my horses and family. I particularly enjoyed seeing the finished product of a subliminal message I deliberately sent to the viewers: it was an idyllic scene showing me riding one of my beautiful Arabians with my youngest child, Ethan, in the saddle in front of me. We were both wearing helmets. I hoped that millions of mothers watching that evening were thinking, "Wow. This woman obviously cares about her children's safety. Maybe she knows what she's talking about, after all."

While that tape was rolling, I got the first words of the story in a voice-over: "I don't have any affinity for guns. It's a tool that can be used to kill a family. It's a tool that can be used to protect a family. But it's just a tool."

Later I reiterated, "It's a hunk of metal. And I will say it again. It merely depends on who is behind it."

Jennings also mentioned that I would be at the Million Mom March the next weekend to make certain that the other point of view would be represented. On tape I said it was "To let the world at large know that these bless-their-hearts, well-intentioned, but completely misguided women do not represent all American women."

I hope it made my family proud.

In the years following the massacre, I have been privileged to have intermittent contact with the guitar god of rock and roll, Ted Nugent, and his absolutely gorgeous (would you expect less?) wife, Shemane. You do not have to meet him in person to have a keen sense of the man. He exudes self-confidence and charisma in one-on-one meetings, just as he does on stage. I am enthralled by the way he teaches and preaches self-reliance and strength from within. Believe me, the man walks the talk. He does not tolerate "wussies."

As I recall the story he shared of his early days, Nugent was going to be the opening act for his own guitar idol, Jimi Hendrix. In the backstage dressing room before the show, Nugent spent some time with the doomed musician. During the encounter, Hendrix offered him some illegal drugs. At that time, so many fans felt it was those drug-induced highs that led to Hendrix's inspired guitar riffs and soulful music. Can you imagine being in Ted's shoes and having your hero offer you drugs? How would you respond?

Ted simply said "No, thanks," and went on to become one of the highest grossing rock stars ever! Dare I also point out that he is still kicking butt, empowering kids, and loudly supporting our Second Amendment rights? Frankly, that impresses the heck out of me.

And Hendrix is, well, dead.

During those years, I participated in more talk shows than I can recall. There are a few that stand out in my mind for various reasons. I know I kept mentioning to my husband that there was really only one I actually *wanted* to be on: "The Phil Donahue Show." At the time, he had one of the few reasonably intelligent programs that used that format. He was notoriously liberal and was known for verbally attacking his guests, but I relished the idea of taking him on.

Then one day, out of the blue, I got the call, and about a week later, I stood at our front door with my suitcase in hand, headed to the airport. My husband kissed me goodbye, and off-handedly said, "Tell Donahue that Bill Corrigan says 'Hi.'"

Bill Corrigan had been the best man at our wedding. My husband had grown up with him in Ohio. I'm sure I blinked a few times, shook my head to clear the fog, and said, "Huh?"

Greg elaborated, "Didn't I mention it to you? Bill's Dad and Phil Donahue were great friends in school. I'm pretty sure the two of them dug the basement of Saint Ed's as a punishment for one thing or another."

"No, Dear. You failed to mention that little bit of information during the MANY times I said I wanted to go on his show! Anything else I should know?"

"No, Honey. Have fun!" So off I went, newly armed with an interesting little morsel of information.

When I arrived at the studio, the employees who do that sort of thing refreshed my makeup and hair. Then, I waited patiently in the Green Room with other guests for what I knew would be a perfunctory meeting with the host. When it was time to head for the staging area, Donahue appeared in the doorway and politely shook hands with each guest as we were shuffled out. When it was my turn, I reached for his hand, introduced myself, and said, "I'm supposed to tell you that Bill Corrigan says, "Hi!" He looked taken aback, so I explained, "He was best man at our wedding."

He immediately brightened, took my outstretched hand in both of his, and said, "How is little Billy?!"

I assured him that "little Billy" was doing fine, briefly explained my husband's connection, and mentioned the fact that Greg had also attended Saint Edward's while growing up in Ohio. Our host went on to tell me that he had not only dug the basement of Saint Ed's with Corrigan's dad, but had shared many a dinner together with their family at one or the other's house.

Needless to say, the tone was changed for the entire show. I mean, how could he attack me or my views now? Not only was I a "victim," but I was practically family! I had been so revved up for a confrontation with this giant of talk-show television, I am not sure that I wasn't a wee bit disappointed in what proved to be a congenial discourse.

As a general rule, stars (the Hollywood type) don't impress me. Please do not misunderstand me: I do not think badly of them simply because they are famous. It is just that the reverse is true: I do not think well of them simply because they are famous. Who DOES impress me is a person who has hit the top rung in their chosen field through hard work, determination, and pure passion for their vocation. I have met quite a few stars. Some I would like to hang out with; some I wouldn't.

Admittedly there are a few who are just larger than life. Merely shaking hands with them or being in their vicinity gives you bragging rights. For me that list would be short and, to the extent that some are deceased, impossible to fulfill. So you can imagine the thrill I got when I found out the NRA was going to have their newly elected president, Charleton Heston, present me with a Life Membership in the association. We were talking about God, Moses, Soylent Green guy (OK, maybe we should skip that one), and Ben Hur (my personal favorite) all rolled into one honest-to-goodness Star.

The presentation was put together in less than two days, and was to take place at a hotel in Dallas at about 6:30 in the morning. Greg and I arrived with baby Ethan in tow. Mr. Heston was just as impressive in person as he was on the big screen. The presentation was quick (maybe twenty minutes), intimate (me, Greg, baby Ethan, and three or four others), and videotaped, so I have proof! Even my parents would have been impressed with that one! Charleton Heston and his movies had always been favorites in our house.

Most radio shows I have done via telephone, but a few have taken place in a studio. One in particular holds a place card in my mind. G. Gordon Liddy, famous Watergate fall guy, has a syndicated talk show on which I was privileged to be an in-studio guest. Mr. Liddy impressed me as a gentleman and genuinely engaging fellow, though with his shaved head, mustache, and leather jacket, he looks like a pretty tough guy. He had a very dry sense of humor I immediately liked. Of course, the subject was the Second Amendment and our right to defend ourselves. Early in the program, he felt it necessary to explain to his listeners, "Now as a convicted felon, I cannot own any guns. But let me tell you that *Mrs.* Liddy has quite an arsenal." Too funny!

When the show was over, and I stood up to leave, my hair got caught up in the headphones. I was slightly embarrassed when Mr. Liddy insisted on delicately untangling me. He gave me a hug, and I left thinking, "I wouldn't mind having that felon as a neighbor!"

CHAPTER 17
The Media Are Your Friends

I have come to a realization that will make many pro-Second Amendment readers mistrust their eyes:

THE MEDIA ARE YOUR FRIENDS.

If you would like to take a break at this point and get yourself a cup of coffee, I will understand. Then come back, sit down and read that line again. I will wait....

I know for anyone on this side of the gun debate, that is going to be a hard pill to swallow. But it is true. You just have to be willing to play their game and play by their rules. Much like a game of cards, playing by the rules will not always get you a win, but it will keep you in the game. And just like in cards, there are things you can do to legitimately tilt the odds a little in your favor. The rules are pretty simple, but only one really matters: with few exceptions, the media exist to make money. I am not talking about the reporters here, I am talking about the newspaper, radio station, broadcast company, magazine, etc. that employs them. It is their ultimate purpose. And you have heard the old adage, "If it bleeds, it leads." Empathy is what brings people together and makes us all feel connected. It is also what sells papers. So perhaps as my brother said, reading or hearing about tragic occurrences brings about feelings of "There but for the grace of God go I" or similar thoughts. Whatever the reasons, victimology sells.

But in the gun debate, it has nearly always been the other side that trots out the victims. Of course, my heart innately goes out to them, and I identify with their pain (Been there, done that!)...right up to the point that they seem to believe that it was the gun that became animated, walked into a room of its own volition, and pulled its own trigger. That is where my empathy is pulled up short.

I have no love of firearms. Don't get me wrong, I can appreciate a beautifully engraved breech, polished wood stock, or the sleek lines of some rifles or antique revolvers. But often, they are just an ugly chunk of metal. To me, mostly, a gun is merely a tool: a very dangerous tool, to be sure, but a tool nonetheless. It is a tool that can be used to kill a family, or a tool that can be used to protect a family. The gun itself has not altered its configuration in those two scenarios, but the intent of the person holding it has made all the difference.

I do not like chainsaws; they scare me. They are heavy, noisy, and very dangerous. I have had more than one patient over the years who have, at least partially, severed their own limbs while using one. (Then, of course, there is the infamous teenage slasher-movie about a crazed nutcase who chops people up with his chainsaw, skins his victims, and sews together the pieces to wear around the house. Yuck!) But, we do own one—a chainsaw, that is. And with a trained and diligent person at the helm, it can quickly help turn a rough piece of property into a showplace. Even after natural disasters like tornados and floods, chainsaws are potential lifesavers, cutting escape hatches in roofs or in collapsed debris, through which people can be pulled to safety.

It is all about who is at the trigger.

If you have paid any attention to the news over the past few decades, you have heard of the horrific use of machetes by mobs or individuals intent on slaughtering innocents. On other continents, men with a twisted sense of justice, cut off the hands and arms of day-old babies as the mothers and siblings helplessly look on. How easily one person with a gun could hold off one hundred people with machetes and protect their families from such madness! There was a very recent case in Uganda in which witnesses said that men armed with machetes, clubs, and swords burst upon a group of over a hundred women and children seeking refuge in a church. By the time they were finished slashing, bludgeoning, and hacking their defenseless victims, aide workers were unable to give an accurate accounting of the dead. There were too many pieces for them to do more than guess at the number. Some said the rebels did it. Some said the Ugandan army did it. I suppose it really doesn't matter. Would the attackers have been so bold if they suspected the mothers could fight back? I doubt it.

The only good that comes from something like this is that, if we are wise, it can serve as a reminder that evil exists in this world. When well-intentioned people suggest that you should "arm yourself with conflict resolution skills," remember that there are those on this Earth who think nothing of cruelty and barbarism and who would grin as they slice your child to pieces before your eyes. Good luck trying to "reason with" them.

We saw a video during the LA riots (that occurred after the Rodney King trial) of an Asian man standing on the rooftop of his family's store, with firearm in hand, holding the rioting mobs at bay. It was only one man and one gun, but theirs was one of the only businesses in the area that was not looted and destroyed.

A Reasonable Tool for Reasonable People

There are people who, although they will not say it openly, really do seem to believe that a gun holds some mystical power — that it could hypnotize its user into doing the work of the devil. A case in point unfolded before me during a college class I was asked to lecture. There was a forty-something-year-old man in the class who had the build of a professional football player. He had heard statistics that led him to believe that family members were more likely to kill each other if there was a gun in the house. In response, I asked if he was married. He was. I asked if, in the many years they had been together, he had ever gotten really, really angry at her. He had. Well then, why, I asked, had he not strangled her or beaten her to death, since he was obviously well equipped to do so.

He thought about it a moment, and then said it was because he was a reasonable man who managed to control his emotions and override any momentary passion or need to use violence. As soon as the words left his lips, I saw his eyebrows lift with a thought. Aha! An epiphany! He recognized that he could easily kill his smaller wife with only his hands and feet. And those tools were, of course, always readily available.

Now interestingly, if murder were his intent and a gun was handy, he may very well have chosen the more efficient tool. But if that were actually to happen, we all know that his wife's murder would have been blamed, not on him, but on the "evil gun" that took over his mind and forced him to pull its trigger. If, on the other hand, the woman used a gun to protect herself from a murderous husband, the incident would be used to bolster the notion that a gun is more often used to kill family members or acquaintances. No one ever checks to see if those cases were the result of self-defense. Unfortunately, rape, assault, and murder are also more often perpetrated by someone who is known to the victim.

I read a short newspaper article two months after the deaths of my parents and shortly before Christmas. It was a terribly sad story about a man who murdered his brother in a moment of insanity during a family argument. His weapon of choice was a Christmas tree stand. He told the officers that it was simply the first thing he could lay his hands on, and in his rage, he used it to bludgeon his sibling to death. There is no doubt in my mind that if a revolver had been sitting on the table next to the tree stand, the article would have been on the front page of that section, instead of buried in the middle. And the gun would have been the culprit. There is also no doubt that the incident would have been used in statistical evidence of how guns (not brothers) kill family members.

Crimes of passion happened well before the advent of the gun, well before Julius Ceasar's day, and will probably continue into eternity. If we could make firearms disappear forever, kings and peasants would still die at the hands of friends, enemies, political foes, acquaintances, and lovers. And, if all the guns did suddenly vaporize, we would actually lose what has been accurately called The Great Equalizer. I have been in countless debates where my well-meaning opponent suggests that, since women are often the victims of violent crimes, they should learn martial arts or carry pepper spray. I agree! Anything that can improve someone's odds against an aggressor should be included in one's bag of tricks or (metaphorical) arsenal.

But, what about the little old grandmother, who is wheelchair-bound and must make the trek to and from her mailbox for her social security check? What happens when those two or three young gang members approach, wielding baseball bats and demanding her money? Should she throw her keys at them? Should she shower them with pepper spray and hope she does not inhale the noxious chemical as she attempts to retreat? Or maybe she could ask them to hold off a moment while she dials 9-1-1?

I do not think those are realistic responses. The one surefire way for that frail, elderly woman to gain equal footing with three, strapping young criminals, is to display a gun.

Yes, but Suzanna, what if one of them has a gun?

Then she must evaluate the situation and make her best guess at the right course of action. There are times when giving up the money may be the best option. However, there are also times when it is not just the money they are after. At least she changes the odds by being armed. Usually criminals do not want to risk being killed either.

We hear so many stories that never made it to the newspaper in which people simply displayed their weapon and the bad guy fled. Oftentimes, the intended victim does not report the incident. After all, what are the cops going to do, write a report about some minor infraction (a perceived threat?) and begin a manhunt? Probably not. And maybe the citizen will get hassled by the police for brandishing a weapon, as my husband was.

There is no way for anyone to really know exactly how the bad guy would have carried through with his crime. Would it have been "just a robbery"? Or would it have ended in kidnapping, rape, or even murder? We will never know, because the attempt was thwarted early in the process. In fact, many people choose not to report incidents because they are not certain of the legality of their chosen method of self defense. Many times, the laws are unclear, or they fear that their names and faces will be smeared all over the news in a less than flattering way.

Ultimately, armchair quarterbacking leads us nowhere. I cannot blame anyone for being unwilling to risk their lives by making the wrong assumption about a criminal's intent.

CHAPTER 18
Rules for Being Interviewed

That leads me to one of many areas in which the media can be of service to Second Amendment believers. Perception can certainly influence reality. As we all know, if a camera crew shows up at your gun show or other gun-related event, they are going to get some camouflage-wearing, front-tooth-missing, white-guy-Bubba to stand in front of their camera and enthusiastically say, "Guns is good!" All of the six and ten o'clock news watchers will have that cliché cemented into their brains, once again. That vision seems to resurface frequently around voting time.

So who *is* the perfect person to shove in front of the camera at firearm events, while someone else is spiriting Bubba far away from the reporters? Warning: Politically correct types may want to avert their eyes from the next sentence. My ideal would be a black, pregnant, lesbian from the inner city, confined to a wheelchair, who does not like the idea of blasting Bambi, but has herself been a victim. She would be the absolute antithesis to the old-white-guy-Bubba-hunter. She is someone who clearly needs the ability to protect herself. More importantly, she will confuse the enemy.

Once you have achieved getting that ideal person—or the nearest thing to it—in front of the reporter, he or she must know the proper words to use. For you see, the other side looks at camouflaged Bubba and uses words like radical, extremist, discriminatory, and racist or, at the very least, implies them. But, in fact it is *their* side that is *radical*—they want to alter the Constitution! Their position is *extremist*—they want to flush two hundred years of tradition down the drain! Their attitude is *discriminatory* at best and *racist* at worst.

If you have any doubt regarding the validity of the last two assertions, I would suggest you do a little light research on your own. You can start with the laws in the "may issue" states[1], where rich white guys in rural counties get to carry, but single black women in the inner-city, high-crime areas who desperately need to protect their families do not. Continue your studies with the history of gun control in this country, which stemmed from the fear of newly freed slaves. You can go from there to the backdoor discrimination that goes on in the "shall issue" states[2], where a class has to be taken and a test passed at a cost of a hundred plus dollars. Then there are fingerprinting and photography fees, and the license itself may cost over a hundred dollars. None of that even takes into consideration the cost of a decent gun. Thus, someone of lesser means is effectively prevented from carrying.

Finally, you can end with reading any of the gazillion accounts of mass genocide that have occurred at any given time and place in the world. You will find these slaughters are nearly always preceded by disarmament, so as to render the victims helpless.

Yes, I think "potentially racist" is not too strong.

Radical. Extremist. Discriminatory at best. Racist at worst. Those terms should be used in reference to gun-control activists for two reasons: because they are accurate, and they get printed.

---

1   *A "may issue" state is one in which a concealed-carry license is issued at the whim of some bureaucrat, often the sheriff or police chief.

2   A "shall issue" state is one in which a concealed-carry license MUST be granted if the legal hoops have been successfully jumped through. Those hoops typically consist of passing a background check, being of legal age, taking a class on the current laws regarding carry and when deadly force is appropriate, passing a written exam, showing proficiency with a handgun, being photographed and fingerprinted, and paying the necessary fees.

There is a potentially fatal flaw in my reasoning. If you are at a gun show when the media arrive, you cannot use those terms if there are vendors who are visibly touting the Ku Klux Klan, Neo-Nazism, or any other hate-filled garbage. While I believe in the First Amendment and their right to speak and display their propaganda, it greatly hurts our cause when it is placed in proximity to firearms.

As much as I enjoy going to gun shows and browsing the booths, I avoid them now as a family affair, simply because I do not want my children to make any false connection between the two. The hate-mongers make up a tiny minority of Second Amendment advocates, just as they make up a fraction of gun-control activists, but they can be made to look as if they represent everyone on our side of the issue. I can promise the cameras will find those booths and make the connection for their viewers.

My unsolicited suggestion to the gun-show producers would be to eliminate those hate mongers from their shows altogether or, at the very least, segregate them — yes, I used that word — to some separate area where my kids do not have to see them, and the cameraman has a hard time including them in a piece about the gun show. I believe more families would frequent the events and bring their wallets with them. My friends and I certainly would.

There is one organization many of you have probably never heard of, but that should be embraced, so to speak, and encouraged to interact with the media and other liberal types. They are called the Pink Pistols: people within the homosexual community who believe in the sacred ability to defend themselves. Their website reads, "Armed gays don't get bashed." Boy, howdy! Regardless of your opinion of their lifestyle choices, they seem to have a firm grasp on the concept of self-preservation and are perfect to use with the press.

Working with the Media

I am pretty sure that when I wrote that the "media are your friends," I heard an audible groan from my readers. But it is true. With the advent of the Internet and email, they are no longer the only game in town, but they are still the ones that get to the masses in a consistent fashion. So you must be willing to play their game! The men and women who are at the other end of the microphones or recorders are, with very few exceptions, just regular people trying to do a job and earn a paycheck. Most respond to genuine friendliness and politeness.

I have found many would-be Second Amendment advocates are scared to death that some evil reporter will deliberately misquote them or trick them into saying something absurd. Although I cannot say this never happens, I don't believe it is typical. Nine out of ten times, they have been sent out on what they consider to be a boring assignment, and they simply need to get a couple of ten-second quotes for the six o'clock news or a few paragraphs of copy for the next day's paper. To that end, they are likely to ask you a couple of painfully simplistic or slightly provocative questions.

The key is simple, à la Neal Knox: you can say whatever you want—or nothing at all! More often than not, the question you are asked will be open-ended. If it is a typical fluff question, answer it, then immediately go on to whatever you want your message to be. If it is interesting or provocative, they will pick up on it and ask a few more leading questions, which will allow you to elaborate.

Those wonderful words...radical, extremist, discriminatory, racist...have a tendency to throw them off guard, since the other side of the gun-control debate has used them against us so adroitly and for so many years. Once you have forced them to take that mental step backward, their minds are briefly opened, and you can use the opportunity to politely educate them. Of course, having the disabled lesbian as your front man, doesn't hurt either.

Another rule of thumb: do not let a microphone or audio recorder intimidate you. Personally, I am comforted by their presence, for I know that I am much more likely to be quoted correctly if one is in use. If you are being interviewed, and a recording device of some sort is not being used, speak your salient points slowly and with the awareness that they are doing their best to jot it down correctly. Do not be afraid to reiterate an important point. If they got it the first time, they will not bore their listeners/readers with repeating it in their medium. If they did not get it, then perhaps they will on the second go around.

They are often thrilled to have someone who is willing to lead the interview in an interesting direction. Therefore, know what direction you want to take it and what points you want to make ahead of time, if possible. It is less work for them, and they will have more material from which to glean their end product. That generally makes them—and their bosses—happy. Win, win!

Every now and then you will get a reporter who really knows what he or she is doing, and they really are out to get you. Stay calm and keep your sense of humor. If you cannot answer the question in the way it was posed to you—for example, "Yes or no, have you stopped beating your wife?" Or, "Do you walk to school, or carry your lunch?"—then simply chuckle and say, "I am not going to answer the question the way you are asking it." When they see you are confident and in control of yourself, they will back off and treat you with more consideration or go looking for some other patsy.

For those of you who, for one reason or another, expect to be in front of a camera repeatedly, I strongly suggest you make friends with the cameramen. They are easy to overlook, because it is not their face that you see on the TV all the time. Moreover, they often do not speak at all but let the reporter rule the roost. However, if it is a local station, there is a good chance the cameraman will be around for many years, whereas the surprisingly low-paid reporters come and go. If the guy on the other end of the lens likes you, he is much more likely to make sure the lighting is good and will let you know if you have broccoli in your teeth or a booger dangling from your nose. Along those lines, if you are a woman, I strongly suggest you ask for a moment to powder your nose. Do not run off to the restroom, but quickly pull out your compact and take off the shine. If you are a man, dab the shine off with a napkin or handkerchief.

If you know ahead of time that you will be on camera, make a point of wearing matte makeup and just touch up the color. I am the Queen of Nose Shine, and I have learned that nothing seems to ding someone's on-camera credibility quicker than an oily shine. The same goes for big, dangly earrings or a crooked tie. If you are a balding man, brush a little powder over your shiny exposed areas for the same reason. There is a reason those anchormen wear makeup, and you want to look just as good on screen as they do!

If you do this sort of thing often enough, there will be days you simply will not be at your best, may even say things that just don't come out right, or just get completely misquoted. All you can do after an interview like that is take a deep breath, learn from it, and look forward to the next one. Chalk it up to experience.

Always be polite. The Golden Rule applies, especially when you consider that you will not be around to give your input at editing time.

❖ ❖ ❖

CHAPTER 19
Affecting
the Law-Making Process

If you desire to be involved with the legislative process, the last couple of rules mentioned in Chapter 17 still apply: always be polite and treat others as you would like to be treated. See? Good points are always worth repeating!

Legislators are just people, like you and I. When they are at home, many of them wear sweatpants or shorts, play with the kids, mop the floors, clean the toilets, and, at least in my case, muck out the stalls. (Of course my husband would say that I shoveled manure in the Capitol as well. The only difference would be the footwear: boots in one place and high heels in the other.) They may have had different upbringings, socioeconomic backgrounds, or philosophies, but in the end they are just people.

I truly believe, particularly at the state level, most of the office holders are there because they want to make life better for their families, friends, and neighbors. Jumping through the hoops necessary to get elected to any high office is not for the faint of heart. It is a grueling ordeal for the candidates and their families. In many, if not most, states, the pay is far less than they could earn by working the same long, hard hours at a private enterprise. The vast majority will tell you they made the jump to public life with one overwhelming conviction: that they could make a positive difference in their world.

That is contrary to a belief seemingly held by many Americans: that most legislators are in office for financial gain or self-aggrandizement. At the state level, at least, my experience leads me to believe otherwise.

It is painfully obvious, however, that the vast majority of elected officials are products of our government education system. That is my not-so-subtle way of telling you they have probably never read the entire Declaration of Independence, Constitution, Bill of Rights, or other documents that should be vital to proper governance in the United States of America.

I think it is criminal that our children waste twelve-plus years in public schools without having taken much more than a passing glance at these papers. In "Legislative Members Only" lounges within the Capitol, I have occasionally asked certain legislators what they thought was the approximate length of the Declaration of Independence. It has embarrassed me to hear everything from thirty to three hundred pages as answers! These are the folks that are creating new laws. I have put the same question to hundreds of high-school students and have rarely gotten the correct answer. Some of those children will become the next generation of lawmakers. For those of you who do not know, the most important document in this country's history is a mere one and one-half pages in length in its original form. *(See the appendices for the text of the Declaration of Independence.)* It is even more disturbing to see senators and representatives on both sides of the aisle stand up and take an oath to uphold the Constitution, which many — most? — have also never read.

I have often thought it would be fun to introduce a bill that would require office holders to pass a simple exam regarding these basic documents before they could take a vote or introduce any legislation. Of course such a bill would never pass, but the squirming it would induce might be fun to watch.

Citizen Lobbying

When getting started with citizen lobbying — and that is what we call constituents working for a cause — the National Rifle Association lobbyist and your local state rifle association governmental liaisons can help you with sound advice that should be followed. There are many good pamphlets and short books on the subject, so I will not go into great detail in this chapter. Most state legislators have pamphlets available that explain the fundamentals and are state-specific.

Learn how the process works, and you will most likely feel much better about what strides we have all made over the last decade in furthering our Second Amendment cause. The law-making process can be very frustrating at times and has been likened to sausage-making: you may not want to know all the details. But do not take your frustrations out on the legislators or their staff. That may end up being the vote you need on a committee, and you could end up being directly responsible for a good bill's death.

I cannot stress the human factor enough. Remember they are not experts in everything on which they take a vote. When a legislator begins a session, the Speaker of the House, Lieutenant Governor, or your state's equivalent will typically place legislators on one or more committees that deal with topics on which they have some knowledge or expertise. It is also possible that the placement has occurred to balance a committee, deliberately unbalance it, or as a punishment for not playing ball when the Speaker or other senior lawmaker deemed it necessary.

Almost every member of the legislature could probably be considered an expert, or at least very knowledgeable, in a few areas. But you should be aware that a representative will take thousands of votes during one session, and many of those votes will be on subjects he knows little about. If that lawmaker is a product of the public education system I discussed earlier, he may very well be sitting on a metaphorical fence when deciding how to vote on a particular bill. Constituents may be calling him, consultants may be texting him, and the Speaker or the Governor may be pressuring him for a specific vote. Each may be pushing him to one side of the fence or the other. The legislator has licked his finger and held it high in the air to see which way the voters will blow it and him.

Phoning ahead for a meeting is a courtesy that will be appreciated and will increase the possibility of getting face time with the lawmaker. Do not expect to get more than fifteen minutes allotted to that meeting. It is not that your representative wouldn't like to take more time with your personal issues, but he has a multitude of other constituents who would like a small piece of him as well. If you are dropping in on him unannounced, it is far more likely you will only get two or three minutes with a staff member. Do not take it personally, but — and I am speaking from experience — during a session, legislators are often expected to be in several places at once: two simultaneous committee meetings, on the phone with a ticked-off superintendent, a reporter on another line, in a conference room with a group that made an actual appointment, and trapped in the hall by two handicapped constituents who have a speaking disorder.

Sometimes walking with the lawmaker to a committee hearing is your best chance to give him a brief pitch. Then politely leave him at the door, and let him know that you will be leaving pertinent information with his staff. He will appreciate your sensitivity and be more likely to shift things around to accommodate you in the future. Remember, he has twenty other constituents watching the proceedings inside the hearing room and wondering where their representative is.

When and if you do get an appointment, regardless of whether it is with the legislator or his staff-person, a box of warm cookies from a local shop for all of the staff is always a nice touch. No, it is not a bribe, but in combination with your charm it may get you an appointment a little bit quicker next time. Be prepared to make a brief presentation that preferably includes a local, pertinent anecdote. The more personal or human you can make it, the better. This is another reminder that he is part of the human race as well, and a factual story involving one of his constituents — read: voters — can be very persuasive.

It is always helpful to leave a one-page, bullet-point flyer for the staff to review at a later time. It should include as many bullets, or one to two sentence snip-its, as necessary to make your point, and have your contact information in bold format at the top. If you leave three pages or more, or the equivalent of a dissertation, it is highly likely it will go unread, unless the representative is a freshman. You may keep that on hand as reference material, but they will ask for more information only if it is necessary, and most of the time it is not. If you cannot get the highlights onto one page, then you are not ready for prime time. Sorry.

A note to the long of wind: when the person making your appointment tells you you will have ten minutes, or fifteen, or five, do not moan, whine, or say something that will put you on the mental "No Future Appointments" list staff all carry in their young little heads. An example of what not to say: "But, I can't even give him the background of the problem in only fifteen minutes!" Once again, if you can't summarize it in five minutes or so, you still need coaching.

If there is a piece of legislation — a bill — that is being taken up for consideration by a committee, the chairman may open the hearing to public testimony. There are a couple of points regarding testifying at those hearings I would like to touch on. I have been on both sides of that podium: I have testified on behalf of improving gun laws in many, many states, and I have sat at the dais as either a member of or chairman of a committee trying to absorb the testimony of dozens of witnesses. It is not uncommon for those legislators to sit for hour after hour listening to incredibly boring testimony about some other representative's bill.

Remember, not everyone has the same interests or passions as you and yours. Let your lobbyist guide you and orchestrate the testimony. If he or she knows they already have the votes for their bill, please do not torture everyone with hours of nearly identical comments, just because you want your five minutes of glory. Please do not get up and repeat what the ten people before you just said! If you have a new point, by all means make it and sit down. If your point is not a new one, fill out the appropriate witness form for or against the bill, turn in a copy of any written testimony you may have, and let the committee complete its work. I promise they will appreciate you for being considerate of their time and will respect your knowledge of the system.

The key is to live to fight another day.

Very often, the lobbyist[1] will have a set of three to six people who will touch on different aspects of a bill. It is a coordinated presentation, and it often works very well. The reasoning is that different approaches work

---

1   A word about lobbyists and special interest groups: they have really gotten a bad rap. Every single one of you has a "special interest" or two. You are obviously somewhat into gun rights. You may also be a real-estate agent, doctor, plumber, engineer, parent with children in government school, etc. You have a vested interest in proposed laws regarding those things that directly affect you and your family. Most people are far too busy earning a living, raising a family, or otherwise living their lives, to acquaint themselves with the intricacies of legislation. So you get together and form an association of like-minded individuals and pay dues. Then it is that association's job to hire a lobbyist to look out for your "special interests." You all have lobbyists working for you in one way or another. They are not The Evil Empire, just hired guns who get paid to protect you while you go about the business of earning a living. Lobbyists know how to do it. They hang around the Capitol all day and night, waiting for legislators to (they hope) take a dinner break. If they want them to listen to all the little details of their clients' issues, then they get more time if it is done over dinner. If they were taking me to dinner (and I was hungry, tired, and stuck away from home), then they would not get away with McDonald's. They also know legislators might not even break for dinner, in which case all of their waiting becomes fruitless…until the next day.

on different committee members. Sometimes more than one technique is needed to get those votes or give the legislators the political cover they need to vote for the bill in question. Most of us political-types like to think we are pretty left-brained decision makers: we use the logical, statistical side of our brain to make those tough voting decisions. The truth is we all make our decisions at the gut level. But we do not want to tell anybody that, so we have to have the statistics to back up what our gut has told us. That is why statistics can be twisted in various ways to make them support what you already want to believe.

A good lobbyist will make certain to have both types of testimony on hand, statistical and emotional, not only for the committee members, but also for the inevitable media who attend gun-control debates. If you are testifying, and unless you are the numbers guy, speak from the heart, quote very few statistics unless you want to put everyone to sleep, and do not read your speech. The members can read just fine and probably faster than you can say it out loud. Feel free to use notes so you do not lose your message to nervousness. Outlines work well for many people. Make sure you have a beginning, a middle, and an end.

Your Testimony Can Make the Difference

Now that I have armed you with a few rules gleaned from being on the voting side of the podium, I must share one very important piece of information: a few times over the years my colleagues and I have sat through hours of duplicative testimony, and our minds were already made up—but hey, the public has a right to speak, right? Then, out of the blue, someone would come to the microphone and say something that turned everything we had heard up to that point on its ear. After some questions and answers, several of us might have drifted to the lounge for a cup of coffee, where we could still hear the testimony, but were out of sight. We might have looked at one another in surprise. One of the representatives might have said, "Wow! Did that change your mind? It sure did mine!"

It might be your testimony that makes all the difference. There may be one fence sitter with whom you make a connection without even knowing it. His may be the deciding vote. So, if you have something different to say, get up and say it.

That covers a few basic rules I believe apply in all fifty states. Do not let the system frustrate you, although Lord knows it can be devilishly frustrating at times. It is a slow and ponderous system. Things could be done much more quickly and efficiently in a dictatorship, but I think the slower version we currently have is preferable. Unless, of course, I get to be the dictator.

The other rule I suggested applying while talking to the media bears repeating for dealing with legislators: be polite. Find out the proper way to address the committee members and do it that way. Every state is a little bit different in that regard. Some use senator, some are representative or assemblyman, some want to be referred to as chairman or madam chair. In a few states, the person testifying must always address the chairman before answering a member's questions. Tradition and rules are important, so when in Rome...you know the rest.

Of course, this is a do-as-I-say-not-as-I-do moment. Since I am often an invited guest to other states, I really try to follow the advice I have given in the previous few paragraphs. But there was one rather infamous bit of testimony I gave that aired on CNN and is still floating around the Internet. No more than two or three days go by that I don't have an acquaintance tell me that they received an email with the attached link.

Years ago I was invited to Washington, D.C., to speak before a House committee that was hearing a bill regarding the proposed assault weapons ban. I was to be part of the first panel that was to include Sarah Brady of Handgun Control, Inc., and her now-wheelchair-bound husband, James Brady, who had been shot in an attempt on President Ronald Reagan's life.

An hour ahead of time the hearing room was packed and television cameras were everywhere. I called my husband and made him a bet that I would be pulled off that panel. I said there was no way they were going to let me sit and speak at the same table as Brady with all of the media there, and Sarah Brady always seemed to manage to avoid debating me.

Sure enough, ten minutes ahead of starting time I was informed that I was moved to the third panel. When I entered the room the number of ugly guns that the committee had laid out on tables in front of the dais overwhelmed me. Not a polished wood stock or engraved barrel in the bunch.

For the next few hours I sat and listened to one person after another, both on the panels and on the committee, refer to the guns before them and say, "This gun has no legitimate hunting purpose." Sarah Brady recounted her husband's terrible tragedy as the cameras rolled and the committeemen leaned forward with keen interest. She also repeated the mantra: "These guns have no legitimate sporting purpose."

One man sat with his small daughter on his lap. His young wife had been killed in a workplace shooting by a man with a so-called assault weapon. My heart went out to both him and his young daughter. But in listening to him, I realized that he really seemed to believe the evil gun had somehow transformed a sane man into committing those horrific murders. How very sad, both for him and for the future self-responsibility of his daughter, that he could not see the illogic in his argument.

As an aside, I happen to know a woman who was also a victim in that very same shooting spree. She told me how she heard the shots and looked out into the hall where she saw the gunman approaching. She pushed a coworker — that little girl's mother perhaps? — back into her office and locked the door...or so she thought. As she was retrieving a pistol from her own purse, he burst through the door and shot them both. Her coworker died, while she was critically injured with a gunshot to the spine. Although she survived, she will spend the rest of her life in a wheelchair.

The committee consisted of several congressmen, but I remember only two: a black man from Illinois, who was not actually a member of that committee, but had been invited to sit in, and Charles Schumer, who I am reasonably sure has "666" tattooed somewhere on his body. More than once I watched Schumer pick up one of the uglier guns, dangle it between his thumb and forefinger as if it were a dead rat, and declare, "This gun has no legitimate sporting purpose!"

The panel on which I was newly placed consisted of then executive director of the NRA's Institute for Legislative Action, Tanya Metaksa; a medical doctor and father who had a fabulous head for statistics; a second doctor who had recently come out with some erroneous statistics showing you are much more likely to get shot if there is a gun in the house (that is like saying you are much more likely to be killed in a car accident if you ever ride in cars); and myself.

When it became my turn to testify, three hours had passed and much of the media had gone, which was an intelligent strategic move on the anti-gunners part. As I told the story of how my parents and twenty others were killed by a madman that day in 1991, I noticed that Schumer was not listening. But it went beyond that. This man who had leaned forward and listened intently to Sarah Brady as she spoke, who would furrow his brow in a possibly feigned attempt to appear distressed at her personal pain, was now leaning back in his chair chit-chatting and chuckling with his aide and even rolled his eyes more than once while I recounted the death of my parents.

While committee members in the past have completely disagreed with my stance on guns, I have never had anyone be so entirely rude and disingenuous as Charles Schumer was that day. As I continued my testimony, I found myself growing more and more angered by his lack of respect and blatant disregard for propriety. I struggled to finish, and as I did, the hair on the back of my neck stood on end.

The Six-Hundred-Pound Gorilla

I paused for several long seconds and glanced at the other panelists. No one was saying what really needed to be said. I looked at the other panelists and thought, *they have jobs to lose over this, but I don't.* So, it fell to me.

When I spoke again, it was to call attention to the six-hundred-pound gorilla in the room: "I've been sitting here, getting more and more fed up with all of this talk about these pieces of machinery having 'no legitimate sporting purpose, no legitimate hunting purpose.' People, that is not the point of the Second Amendment! The Second Amendment is not about duck hunting. And, I know I'm not going to make very many friends saying this, but it's about our rights—all of our rights—and I swept my hand over the audience behind me—to be able to protect ourselves from all of you guys up there."

Holy cow, did I open a can of worms? The room erupted into applause that had to be interrupted by the chairman. Then, the invited black—African-American, Negro, person-of-color, or whatever we are calling my darker-skinned brethren these days—congressman redressed me with a comment about my lack of respect for the people on the dais.

Point of interest: that congressman was later convicted of several felonies, including having sex with a sixteen-year-old campaign worker, solicitation of child pornography, obstruction of justice, and a few other ethical gems. President Clinton, during a last minute binge, commuted his sentence.

Apparently my momentary lack of good judgment aired repeatedly on CNN, and I was suddenly and unexpectedly swamped with fan mail. So, instead of lacking judgment, perhaps my sixth sense knew that clear and direct words should be used upon occasion. The elephant in the room, aka the Second Amendment, should not be overlooked, even if it is not politically correct to speak of such archaic principles.

Which leads us back to the topic of public education, or the lack thereof.

CHAPTER 20
Zero Tolerance
for Self-Defense

The Second Amendment is considered by many people to be an outdated concept that, while appropriate two hundred years ago, has no place in our current, civilized society. They have typically come to believe that dangerous lie, simply because it is part of the indoctrination they receive in most of our government schools. If you care to do a little survey on your own, ask some public-education kids a few simple questions about the right to keep and bear arms. Then ask some private-school and home-school kids the same questions. I think you will be shocked at the different answers you will get. The vast majority of our future employees, business owners, legislators, and voters will be products of our government indoctrination camps.

Oops. That sounded a bit radical.

We can spend a great deal of time making little in-roads with our legislators and the media. But, it is in the classroom that hearts and minds will be won *en masse*. It was Hitler who said, "He alone, who owns the youth, owns the future." He nearly did. When considering Nazi Germany, it is hard to grasp how regular people could be filled with such lies and genuine hatred for another race of people. Yet when you look at the footage of the indoctrination that occurred in Hitler's government-run schools, it begins to make sense. Kids are such little sponges during those early years, but as they grow up they become part of the future governing bodies. Scary, isn't it?

My family and children are fortunate. Although my sons attend a public school—there are no established private schools within fifty miles of us—we are in a rural area that still believes in Mom, apple pie, and the Second Amendment. However, the drivel that falls from the

mouths of suburban and inner-city teachers and administrators appalls me. When I read stories of an excellent
instructor being fired and subsequently sued because
she used a tiny, neon-colored squirt gun to keep her students awake and to ingrain a valuable physics lesson, I
am concerned. When elementary children are suspended
for forming a gun with their thumb and index finger and
saying, "Pow!" I am concerned. When a straight "A" high-
school student gets expelled because a steak knife is found
in the bed of his pickup after he helped move his grandmother, I am concerned.

Even in our own community, when my child comes
home with the understanding that he is not allowed to
defend himself, I am very concerned. That seems to be a
new drum that all of the schools are beating: zero toler-
ance of fighting. My sons have never been in any fights
except with each other, but I am trying to make it clear
to them that if someone else starts it, and the teachers in
attendance cannot or will not fix it, they always have the
right to defend themselves. Believe it or not, they did not
know that, because our schools have preached otherwise.

Self-defense seems like such a basic concept I thought
everybody understood and agreed with it. I have apparently raised eyebrows in interviews when I have said, "Let
me make this perfectly clear. If I wake up in the middle
of the night, and someone who should not be there is in
my house, I am not turning on the lights to see what color
they are. I am not going to ask how old they are. I will
not question them on whether they are there to rape and
murder my children and me or just steal the television to
support a drug habit. I am pulling the trigger. If the lights
go on, and I see it is a tall fourteen-year-old, I will feel sad
for a moment, but I will not lose nearly as much sleep as if
he had harmed my children. It is incumbent upon me as a
parent to keep my children safe. I will not risk their lives
in the name of political correctness."

I remember being a guest on a radio show during which I said something along those lines. I hardly knew how to respond when a female caller said that she just wasn't sure she could kill someone, even to protect her children. I think I only barely concealed my simultaneous horror and fear for her kids. I ended it by telling her that I pitied her children, and that even a goose would protect its young.

I am not sure she appreciated my insight.

Although time spent picking at firearms laws may be worthwhile, I believe it would be more worthwhile to spend our energy requiring government-run schools to correctly teach the founding of our nation and to spend months—not minutes—reviewing the writings upon which our country is based. If we are to have government schools at all—the intelligence of that design I have come to question more and more deeply—then they should be forced to require a few things at graduation: their students should be able to read, write, do basic math, have a grasp of history, and know our founding documents.

That, my friends, will ensure that Freedom will still coexist with the United States when my grandchildren make an entrance into this world. Legislation, on the other hand, can change with the representative scenery. It would be nice to have assurance that those elected folks were steeped in the basics, wouldn't it? Therefore, the schools require our time and extra efforts. It is in those halls that America and our Second Amendment rights will eventually be won or lost.

EPILOGUE

I have not had any of those weird dreams where my gun jams at the wrong time since the day after my parents were murdered. I wonder if those dreams were, in fact, premonitions of some sort. I am not given to thinking in the fourth dimension or applying too much meaning to things that may just be mere coincidence. I find it odd and interesting, nonetheless, to have spent so many years experiencing that repetitious quasi-nightmare, only to have it abruptly disappear after that incident.

I kept the torn dress and the blood-splattered purse that I had with me that day. I cannot tell you why. The rip in the material is irreparable, and I could not get all of the dark stains off the leather handbag. But, I just cannot bring myself to part with them. My mother's little silver, Indian-feather earrings shined up like new, and I wear them often.

Throughout the last several years of being a vocal gun-rights proponent, one of my biggest fears was (and continues to be) that of being attacked and somehow not able to use my gun for defense. The fear is not just for my safety and well being. It stems from a larger concern that the opponents of our Second Amendment would plaster my death or injuries all over the media, with some silly pronouncement like, "See? Suzanna Hupp's gun couldn't protect her."

Allow me to preempt that possibility, and loudly declare once again, "Guns are not a guarantee. But they sure as heck change the odds!"

To all of the young women, mothers, and grandmothers who may be reading this book with some trepidation…some lingering fear that guns are the devil's creation…please let me assure you I am not into blasting Bambi, either. I am definitely not a hunter. I love almost everything about the hunting experience: being outdoors, observing the wildlife, shooting guns, and playing cards 'til all hours. I am just not into the part about taking a life or being the cause of suffering. Knowing how to hunt, however, could prove to be an invaluable tool. I am a big supporter of hunters' rights, even though I am not personally into the sport.

The one thing that my squeamish readers should understand is that predators exist. Not the hunters that I mentioned in the previous paragraph, but the kind we do not like to think about. I also do not mean robbers or burglars or purse-snatchers. I am talking about people whose brains function in sick and twisted ways normal folks cannot fathom. I am speaking of the real-life nightmares many families have had to endure. Evil exists in this world. Although I don't want you or your children to live in fear, I think the Boy Scout credo is still potentially life-saving: be prepared. Does locking your doors at night mean you are paranoid? Most people don't think so. Do you believe your home will catch on fire anytime soon? Probably not, but you still keep batteries in your smoke alarms, don't you? If you are smart, you and your children may even rehearse an escape route in the event that such a catastrophe befalls you. They have always had fire drills at school, but now they practice "lock downs," as well.

School shootings are still extremely rare, but I am glad administrators are taking precautions and providing the teachers and students a course of action to take in such an unlikely event. Are they trying to scare everybody? I don't think so. I think they are doing their best, within the current law, to ensure their charges' safety. Immediately before and after the recent spate of devastating hurricanes, even the government reminded the public to stay prepared and have a plan.

When it comes to making plans to repel a personal attack on themselves or their family, the average adult falls short. For some bizarre, cultural reason, that kind of pre-paredness is considered paranoid. Yet, unlike house fires or school shootings, every adult in this country has either been the victim of personal crime or knows someone who has.

If you are still unsure of your opinion regarding our Second Amendment, or about your neighbor's right to own and carry a gun, I would like you to ponder this:

Imagine yourself enjoying the last of your lunch in a busy cafeteria on a bright, sunny day. Only, instead of your parents, you are there with your children or grandchildren. A man walks through the door by himself and pauses for a moment to survey the room. You notice him because he is wearing a coat that strikes you as being a bit too heavy for such lovely weather. But it's a subconscious thought, and your attention is pulled back to the conversation.

Sudden movement out of the corner of your eye causes you to snap your head back in his direction. The man yanks open his jacket and stuffs his hands into its folds. As if in a dream, you see him withdraw not one, but two handguns, which he immediately fires into the chest of an elderly woman standing just a few feet to his left. Your jaw drops open, and your eyes grow wide with shock. You cannot believe what you have just witnessed. But he has not finished…he turns and shoots the woman behind the cash register, squarely between the eyes. He starts to walk, calmly and deliberately executing the patrons nearest to him, who have been frozen with fear.

Of course this is not 1991, and many of these terrible shootings have occurred since then. So, you quickly recognize it for what it is. You scan the room for an exit, but there is not one within reach; so you huddle your little children behind you, using your own body as their shield. But he has moved much closer. He executes the young man across the aisle, whom you overheard earlier discussing his upcoming wedding. The nearness of the brutality makes your three-year-old spring forward to cling to your side.

The sudden movement in his peripheral vision catches the madman's attention, and he wheels around to face you. His malevolent grin sends a chill down your spine, and you instinctively pull your child in closer. There is no time for karate, pepper spray, or conflict resolution. He continues with very slow and deliberate movements; the embodiment of evil standing before you brings his smoking weapon down to within inches of your toddler's forehead. At that moment, there is only one question for you to answer:

Even if you have chosen not to carry a gun, don't you hope the guy behind you has one and knows how to use it?

APPENDICES

The Declaration of Independence: A Transcription

IN CONGRESS, July 4, 1776.

The unanimous Declaration of the thirteen united States of America,

When in the Course of human events, it becomes necessary for one people to dissolve the political bands which have connected them with another, and to assume among the powers of the earth, the separate and equal station to which the Laws of Nature and of Nature's God entitle them, a decent respect to the opinions of mankind requires that they should declare the causes which impel them to the separation.

We hold these truths to be self-evident, that all men are created equal, that they are endowed by their Creator with certain unalienable Rights, that among these are Life, Liberty and the pursuit of Happiness.--That to secure these rights, Governments are instituted among Men, deriving their just powers from the consent of the governed, --That whenever any Form of Government becomes destructive of these ends, it is the Right of the People to alter or to abolish it, and to institute new Government, laying its foundation on such principles and organizing its powers in such form, as to them shall seem most likely to effect their Safety and Happiness. Prudence, indeed, will dictate that Governments long established should not be changed for light and transient causes; and accordingly all experience hath shewn, that mankind are more disposed to suffer, while evils are sufferable, than to right themselves by abolishing the forms to which they are accustomed. But when a long train of abuses and usurpations, pursuing invariably the same Object evinces a design to reduce them under absolute Despotism, it is their right, it is their duty, to throw off such Government, and to provide new Guards for their future security.--Such has been the patient sufferance of these Colonies; and such is now the necessity which constrains them to alter their former Systems of Government. The history of the present King of Great Britain is a history of repeated injuries and usurpations, all having in direct object the establishment of an absolute Tyranny over these States. To prove this, let Facts be submitted to a candid world.

He has refused his Assent to Laws, the most wholesome and necessary for the public good.

He has forbidden his Governors to pass Laws of immediate and pressing importance, unless suspended in their operation till his Assent should be obtained; and when so suspended, he has utterly neglected to attend to them.

He has refused to pass other Laws for the accommodation of large districts of people, unless those people would relinquish the right of Representation in the Legislature, a right inestimable to them and formidable to tyrants only.

He has called together legislative bodies at places unusual, uncomfortable, and distant from the depository of their public Records, for the sole purpose of fatiguing them into compliance with his measures.

He has dissolved Representative Houses repeatedly, for opposing with manly firmness his invasions on the rights of the people.

He has refused for a long time, after such dissolutions, to cause others to be elected; whereby the Legislative powers, incapable of Annihilation, have returned to the People at large for their exercise; the State remaining in the mean time exposed to all the dangers of invasion from without, and convulsions within.

He has endeavoured to prevent the population of these States; for that purpose obstructing the Laws for Naturalization of Foreigners; refusing to pass others to encourage their migrations hither, and raising the conditions of new Appropriations of Lands.

He has obstructed the Administration of Justice, by refusing his Assent to Laws for establishing Judiciary powers.

He has made Judges dependent on his Will alone, for the tenure of their offices, and the amount and payment of their salaries.

He has erected a multitude of New Offices, and sent hither swarms of Officers to harrass our people, and eat out their substance.

He has kept among us, in times of peace, Standing Armies without the Consent of our legislatures.

He has affected to render the Military independent of and superior to the Civil power.

He has combined with others to subject us to a jurisdiction foreign to our constitution, and unacknowledged by our laws; giving his Assent to their Acts of pretended Legislation:

For Quartering large bodies of armed troops among us:

For protecting them, by a mock Trial, from punishment for any Murders which they should commit on the Inhabitants of these States:

For cutting off our Trade with all parts of the world:

For imposing Taxes on us without our Consent:

For depriving us in many cases, of the benefits of Trial by Jury:

For transporting us beyond Seas to be tried for pretended offences

For abolishing the free System of English Laws in a neighbouring Province, establishing therein an Arbitrary government, and enlarging its Boundaries so as to render it at once an example and fit instrument for introducing the same absolute rule into these Colonies:

For taking away our Charters, abolishing our most valuable Laws, and altering fundamentally the Forms of our Governments:

For suspending our own Legislatures, and declaring themselves invested with power to legislate for us in all cases whatsoever.

He has abdicated Government here, by declaring us out of his Protection and waging War against us.

He has plundered our seas, ravaged our Coasts, burnt our towns, and destroyed the lives of our people.

He is at this time transporting large Armies of foreign Mercenaries to compleat the works of death, desolation and tyranny, already begun with circumstances of Cruelty & perfidy scarcely paralleled in the most barbarous ages, and totally unworthy the Head of a civilized nation.

He has constrained our fellow Citizens taken Captive on the high Seas to bear Arms against their Country, to become the executioners of their friends and Brethren, or to fall themselves by their Hands.

He has excited domestic insurrections amongst us, and has endeavoured to bring on the inhabitants of our frontiers, the merciless Indian Savages, whose known rule of warfare, is an undistinguished destruction of all ages, sexes and conditions.

In every stage of these Oppressions We have Petitioned for Redress in the most humble terms: Our repeated Petitions have been answered only by repeated injury. A Prince whose character is thus marked by every act which may define a Tyrant, is unfit to be the ruler of a free people.

Nor have We been wanting in attentions to our Brittish brethren. We have warned them from time to time of attempts by their legislature to extend an unwarrantable jurisdiction over us. We have reminded them of the circumstances of our emigration and settlement here. We have appealed to their native justice and magnanimity, and we have conjured them by the ties of our common kindred to disavow these usurpations, which, would inevitably interrupt our connections and correspondence. They too have been deaf to the voice of justice and of consanguinity. We must, therefore, acquiesce in the necessity, which denounces our Separation, and hold them, as we hold the rest of mankind, Enemies in War, in Peace Friends.

We, therefore, the Representatives of the united States of America, in General Congress, Assembled, appealing to the Supreme Judge of the world for the rectitude of our intentions, do, in the Name, and by Authority of the good People of these Colonies, solemnly publish and declare, That these United Colonies are, and of Right ought to be Free and Independent States; that they are Absolved from all Allegiance to the British Crown, and that all political connection between them and the State of Great Britain, is and ought to be totally dissolved; and that as Free and Independent States, they have full Power to levy War, conclude Peace, contract Alliances, establish Commerce, and to do all other Acts and Things which Independent States may of right do. And for the support of this Declaration, with a firm reliance on the protection of divine Providence, we mutually pledge to each other our Lives, our Fortunes and our sacred Honor.

There were 56 signatories to the Declaration.

http://www.archives.gov/exhibits/charters/declaration_transcript.html

The Bill of Rights:
A Transcription

The Preamble to The Bill of Rights

Congress of the United States
begun and held at the City of New-York, on
Wednesday the fourth of March, one thousand seven hundred and eighty nine.

THE Conventions of a number of the States, having at the time of their adopting the Constitution, expressed a desire, in order to prevent misconstruction or abuse of its powers, that further declaratory and restrictive clauses should be added: And as extending the ground of public confidence in the Government, will best ensure the beneficent ends of its institution.

RESOLVED by the Senate and House of Representatives of the United States of America, in Congress assembled, two thirds of both Houses concurring, that the following Articles be proposed to the Legislatures of the several States, as amendments to the Constitution of the United States, all, or any of which Articles, when ratified by three fourths of the said Legislatures, to be valid to all intents and purposes, as part of the said Constitution; viz.

ARTICLES in addition to, and Amendment of the Constitution of the United States of America, proposed by Congress, and ratified by the Legislatures of the several States, pursuant to the fifth Article of the original Constitution.

Note: The following text is a transcription of the first ten amendments to the Constitution in their original form. These amendments were ratified December 15, 1791, and form what is known as the "Bill of Rights."

Amendment I

Congress shall make no law respecting an establishment of religion, or prohibiting the free exercise thereof; or abridging the freedom of speech, or of the press; or the right of the people peaceably to assemble, and to petition the Government for a redress of grievances.

Amendment II

A well regulated Militia, being necessary to the security of a free State, the right of the people to keep and bear Arms, shall not be infringed.

Amendment III

No Soldier shall, in time of peace be quartered in any house, without the consent of the Owner, nor in time of war, but in a manner to be prescribed by law.

Amendment IV

The right of the people to be secure in their persons, houses, papers, and effects, against unreasonable searches and seizures, shall not be violated, and no Warrants shall issue, but upon probable cause, supported by Oath or affirmation, and particularly describing the place to be searched, and the persons or things to be seized.

Amendment V

No person shall be held to answer for a capital, or otherwise infamous crime, unless on a presentment or indictment of a Grand Jury, except in cases arising in the land or naval forces, or in the Militia, when in actual service in time of War or public danger; nor shall any person be subject for the same offence to be twice put in jeopardy of life or limb; nor shall be compelled in any criminal case to be a witness against himself, nor be deprived of life, liberty, or property, without due process of law; nor shall private property be taken for public use, without just compensation.

Amendment VI

In all criminal prosecutions, the accused shall enjoy the right to a speedy and public trial, by an impartial jury of the State and district wherein the crime shall have been committed, which district shall have been previously ascertained by law, and to be informed of the nature and cause of the accusation; to be confronted with the witnesses against him; to have compulsory process for obtaining witnesses in his favor, and to have the Assistance of Counsel for his defence.

Amendment VII

In Suits at common law, where the value in controversy shall exceed twenty dollars, the right of trial by jury shall be preserved, and no fact tried by a jury, shall be otherwise re-examined in any Court of the United States, than according to the rules of the common law.

Amendment VIII

Excessive bail shall not be required, nor excessive fines imposed, nor cruel and unusual punishments inflicted.

Amendment IX

The enumeration in the Constitution, of certain rights, shall not be construed to deny or disparage others retained by the people.

Amendment X

The powers not delegated to the United States by the Constitution, nor prohibited by it to the States, are reserved to the States respectively, or to the people.

Note: The capitalization and punctuation in this version is from the enrolled original of the Joint Resolution of Congress proposing the Bill of Rights, which is on permanent display in the Rotunda of the National Archives Building, Washington, D.C.

http://www.archives.gov/exhibits/charters/bill_of_rights_transcript.html

Letter Concerning the Fourth Amendment from Al Gratia to an El Paso Newspaper

"Says Supreme Court's search ruling wrong"

"The recent Supreme Court decision to allow "reasonable" searches, including strip searches of students and their possessions without warrant, is appalling.

"A couple of lawsuits already have entered the system wherein the litigants, young girls, have been stripped in searches for dope. One, a 16-year-old, had no history of drug involvement and no disciplinary history. She is an honor student.

"But, whether good student or not, the Constitution equally applies to all citizens. The meaning of the Fourth Amendment is that no search can be reasonable unless it is backed by an accuser, probable cause, a signed warrant and a description of the person, place and things to be seized.

"This new interpretation gives school authorities power that even the police do not now have. The next step will be to extend this power of warrantless arrest to other authorities.

"What we now have is a situation that licenses school staffs to violate constitutional rights. To get at a few losers, a whole generation of decent young people who don't fool with dope will be educated to the effect that it is all right to renounce the Constitution.

"All searches are degrading. A strip search is de-humanizing. Stripping was used by the enemy in Korea as a prelude to brainwashing. It is particularly horrible in dealing with young people, especially girls.

"Sure, there is a drug and discipline problem that has to be corrected. But find a constitutional way.

"Poor kids. Poor America."